1999

With My Hands Full

Con Mis Manos Llenas

With My Hands Full

Con Mis Manos Llenas

Por los Abrecaminos—

those who make a way
Young Latino Writers in Yakima

Edited by Jim Bodeen

Blue Begonia Press   •   Yakima, WA

Acknowledgments

The stories and poems in this book were written by writers enrolled in a year-long Latino literature and writing course at Davis High School, in Yakima, Washington using bilingual texts from the great works of Latin American writers.

This book would not be possible without the dedicated and committed teachers of Davis where the stories and poems in this book were first created. Everyone who works at Davis works first as a teacher. For over thirty years it has attracted a staff interested in, and committed to, curriculum as well as to the students.

The creation of this book was made possible through the help of many people: Phil Garrison, poet, essayist, professor at Central Washington University, helped me with the original reading list in the early stages of the creation of the course. His time in our classroom contributed to my own development, along with teaching students the great lessons of literature. His contribution remains part of the vision. Jim Rigney's vision sparked this course from the beginning. He is the *garrapata* that makes the difference. Administrators: Gloria de Martinez and Karen Garrison. During difficult times of materials selection, Frank Naasz had one request: *tell me what you need*. The English Department of this school has consistently fought for books and ideas, especially Barry Grimes and Linda Brown; and it has led all of the students in believing that their own words, their search for their own voices, is their most powerful ally in their quest for an education. The work of Gavicel Antúñez and Alma Varela was written with the guidance of Barry Grimes. Sue Grimshaw, Marty Lovins, Rob Prout, in the Art Department, artists all. The course has had the support of many others. Our language department, along with the English as a Second Language program, has always been about the creation of a world community. Raúl Torres, my *compa* from Texas, has become the *abuelo espiritual* of countless Latino students for nearly 30 years, and has led them in the classroom and through MEChA, many times as the only light they had. For our proofreaders, Jorge Rodríguez, Jim Rigney, and Ricardo Martinez, mil gracias. Finally, many thanks to our abogado, Jerry Talbott, for the contract protecting the writers. Karen, *por su puesto*.

The beauty and intellectual diligence with which these students have contributed to my own growth as a person cannot be minimized. Alma Varela. Yoshimi Varela. Javier Vargas. Juan Ortega. Angel Ayon. Omar Ramíriz. They have contributed to my maturity as a person and my recovery as a man. The gratitude I owe them is immense.

Copyright 1999 by Blue Begonia Press and by the writers.
All rights reserved.

Front Cover art by Javier Vargas
Back Cover art by Cesar Vaquera
Illustrations by Rafael Villalobos and Jorge Sánchez
Photographs of writers by Jim Bodeen

ISBN: 0-911287-33-7

Blue Begonia Press   225 South 15th Avenue   Yakima, Washington 98902

for the Abrecaminos
&
Raúl "Torito" Torres

Table of Contents

Preface — Jim Bodeen — 11

Part I Personal Stories

Being An Abrecaminos	Raúl Chacón	17
My Story	René Guzmán	18
Past & Present	Antonio Avila	20
Sixteen and Older	Sandra Abúndiz	21
How I Came to Yakima	Raúl Chacón	23
My Story	Gabino Salazar	25
I See My World Through Your Eyes	Angel Ayon	29
Fearfulness in Life: Omar's Journal	Omar Ramírez	32
A Personal Statement	Rafael Villalobos	38
When I Decided to Come to U.S.	Angel González	40
La Ilusión	Martha Ponce	42

Part II Interviews with Our Mothers & Fathers

My Mom's Interview	Cesar Vaquera	47
Two Sisters Write About Their Mother	Maira Cárdenas and Adriana Cárdenas	53
From a Town Called "Xaloctoc"	Teresa Roque	57
Interview with My Mother	Ricardo Acevedo	60
Background	Juan Romo	64
Celsa, Mi Madre	Omar Ramíriz	70
Enrique Castañeda Torres	Salvador Castañeda Muñiz	73
The Interview	Natalia Castañeda	76
Interview with Natalio Roque	Teresa Roque	78
Jesús Gil Navarro	Jesús Gil	80
From My Uncle to the World	Raúl Chacón	82
Interview with My Mother	Eva Siddhartha Valdivia	84

Part III Poems

Looking for America	Salvador Sánchez	93
53d Birthday	Alma Varela	94
Transportation	Alma Varela	95
Opposites	Alma Varela	97
Like This	Alma Varela	98

Soccer Game	Alma Varela	96
From Gavicel's Poetry Notebook	Gavicel Antunez	100
Mystery	Gavicel Antunez	103
My Grandma's Favorite Gorditas	Beatriz Díaz	104
Just a Few Words	Samuel Barrera	106
Believe In Me	Jacqueline Hernández	108
Why Did You Leave?	Jacqueline Hernández	109
My Pen Is My Voice	René Guzmán	111
The Trip Looking for My Life	Carlos Gonzalez	112
Three Letter Poems to Three Latinas	Carlos Gonzalez	113
La Soledad	Omar Ramírez Cruz	118
Siddhartha Eva	Siddhartha Eva Valdivia	119
Rosa Permanente	Omar Ramíriz	120

Part IV. Macchu Picchu

Going Up to Go Down	Jim Bodeen	123
The Curves of My Life	Rubén Mendoza	125
Adios a Mi Niñez	Javier Vargas	131
Exiting the Old	Angel Ayon	142
Acid Silence	Juan Ortega	151

Part V Short Stories

The World	Citlamina Caltenco	163
Remembering A Friend	Salvador Castañeda Muñiz	169
Why Me?	Luis Solis	172
Young Thoughts	Berenice Garcia	175
Sueños, Dreams, y Recuerdos	Pablo López	177

Part VI A Final Story

Eva Siddhartha Valdivia	Eva Siddhartha Valdivia	181

Part VII About the Authors & Vocabulario   201

Preface

One of the writers in this book who inspires me, and who is responsible for the creation of this book, recently called from Seattle. He is one of the artists in this book, too. He said, "I was thirteen when they brought me here. I was so innocent. I didn't have any choice, but to come." One of his poems in this book won the Reflections Contest in Yakima and went on to become a finalist in the State Reflections Contest.

He is completely bilingual and bicultural. Because he is in a handful of my top students over a long teaching career, I make the claim he is among the best this society can produce. He belongs to us.

When I told Senator Patty Murray about this young man, and others like him, I was told, by Senator Murray and her office, "Tell them to go back to Mexico and try to begin the process from there. There is nothing we can do."

We call ourselves the abrecaminos. Abre means to open. Caminos means paths. Open the ways. Many paths. Each person who makes a way makes many paths. We don't know how we're going to make our road, we only know that's what we're going to do. Make a way. We're not the only ones. Somos muchos. I was given the concept of the abrecaminos by the poet Inés Hernandez. It has turned into one of the guiding principios of my life.

Many of these writers come from the State of Michoacán. Many of them are rural. But many come from the cities too. It is wondrous to me that students come from such great cities as Morelia, Guadalajara, and Mexico City, to put down new roots in Granger, Wapato and Yakima. And many of these writers are Chicano, born here, en este lado de la frontera. They're making their trip the other way. They're going back. These writers cross both ways, making worlds, often inside the borders others only see as dividing lines.

We tell stories and we write them. We read the best Latino texts in bilingual editions. Because so many of these writers have had their lives interrupted, through sudden, and sometimes violent, change, that has never been explained in legitimate contexts, we study the roots of our pasts—nuestras raíces—at the same time we go forward. It's not a course of study. It's a mountain that's been given us to climb. *What are your metaphors?* That's the first question asked. Without the right metaphors, you just might not make this journey. It's not a simulation.

For the past eight years in this course I have used Pablo Neruda's long poem, Las Alturas de Macchu Picchu as the first serious part of the journey. We use this long 12-part poem as a guide to write our own 12-part poems of discovery and transformation. We come to understand the muertes pequeñas, the little deaths that hit us daily, along with the big ones. Four of these long poems are included as a central part of this book, and indeed, there would be no book without these poems.

At the same time, it seems to make more sense to place them toward the center of the book, giving the reader time to catch up, to get to know something of where these writers are coming from and where they've been. They're young, 17, 18, 19 years old, but they bring experience beyond, and outside, any curriculum. I hope, too, that beginning the book with personal stories can help the reader enter into her own story, or his own life journey. Macchu Picchu makes more sense when one is looking at himself alongside a big mountain. We go up to go down. Some of the principles of this part of our trip are included in a brief essay at the beginning of the Macchu Picchu poems. The boy dies and the man is born. Or, as Francisco put it this year, putting his poster on the wall, after arriving at the top, (which is really only a beginning), "Don't let the boy die, let the man be stronger."

After we finish the Macchu Picchu part of the journey, we're ready to study the archetypal images of women in Latino culture. Beginning with Malinche and La Virgen de Guadalupe, we uncover more images than we can study. And we read and write about these women, going on to explore Sor Juana, Rosario Castellanos, Rigoberta Menchú, Laura Esquivel, Sandra Cisneros and Gloria Anzaldúa, before arriving at, and interviewing, our mothers and fathers. That these interviews are also included before the Macchu Picchu poems, is an attempt to show how much we love and value those who have brought us this far, those who were also abrecaminos from necessity, without having been given the honor of the word. All of the women show us how to make way. Rosario Castellanos challenges us to find otro manera de ser. As new beings looking for another way to be and become. This is part of the journey.

So many things. An uprooted, and primarily oral culture, faces technology and the blitz of the media culture.

Look at this Mexican refrane, "Cada vez que muere un anciano se destruye una biblioteca." *Every time an old person dies, a library burns.* As the stories have come through our classroom, we have added the interviews with mothers and fathers to try and save a glimpse of what is being lost during the present migration, a migration that includes technology as well as miles, language, borders and cultural traditions.

If we don't save our mother's stories who will?

Working with these young writers is good work. It's a gift I receive daily. I am a guide along the way. One of many guides. The stories and poems in this book make the claim that curriculum can effect transformational results. The stories are presented as evidence and fact.

In Juan Rulfo's *Pedro Páramo*, the revolutionaries show up at the patrón's house to change the world order and he asks them what they need. He'll give it to them. And when the revolutionaries ask him what they should do, he says, "Join up with the side that's winning." It brings to my mind the current educational reform. Let the current group of educational reformers call up the following writers: Pablo Neruda, Octavio Paz, Eduardo Galeano, Sor Juana Inés de la Cruz, Rosario Castellanos, Juan Rulfo, Laura Esquivel, Gloria Anzaldúa, Tomás Rivera, Rudolfo Anaya, Sandra Cisneros and Alberto Ríos.

Supreme Court Justice William O. Douglas and poet and short story writer Raymond Carver are among the graduates from our school. Memorial plaques and books remember them. Justice Douglas' words remind us every day: "We need be bold and adventuresome in our thinking to survive. The Constitution guarantees freedom of thought and expression to everyone in our society. All are entitled to it...and none needs it more than the teacher." From Carver, at our school,

Davis High School: *This is where I'm calling from.*

That's where I'm calling from, too. What we do with the language comes from poetry. Here it is.

Finally, to the writers. Your stories here are life giving. But we know, too. For every story, there are 100 stories not included. We know the names of those not included. Find a way to remember each name.

Jim Bodeen
Davis High School
Yakima, Washington
Spring, 1999

I. Personal Stories

It's a place in your heart that you won't get to understand unless you see or experience.

Citlamina Caltenco

Being An Abrecaminos

Raúl Chacón

Being an abrecaminos isn't a way of salvation, it's a way of overcoming. Depending on what you think, positive or negative. But if you think negative, don't call yourself an abrecaminos. You better call yourself a cierracaminos.

I consider myself an abrecaminos in many ways. Everyday of the week is the same for me because there are no empty holes in my life. All of them are full of love. Every morning I open my eyes and say, "How wonderful it is to be alive. This day is better than yesterday." Another way to be an abrecaminos is beating every negative thing on me. My parents taught me responsibility and respect toward people, especially women. When I became an abrecaminos I learned the value of everything, and also started taking better control of my acts because if I acted without thinking there will always be something wrong.

When a teacher told me about the abrecaminos word I did not think much about this word, but later this wonderful word helped me in many ways. Being an abrecaminos I discovered friendship, love, hope, desire to be alive, and millions of beautiful things, like during night, I don't sleep. I dream.

My Story

René Guzmán

We were heading north, me and my family. My father said we were heading en busca de una mejor vida. He said, "Estoy cansado de vivir esta vida, cansado de ver a mi familia trabajando estas tierras, tierras que estan cansadas de darnos su fruto. But I'm sure that one day I'm going to rest here just like my ancestors did and I know my sons will."

Tired of sitting in this bus, my eyes are looking at every sign in the road. I see a sign that says, "Tijuana 10 miles." My family is looking at the sign with sad smiles. I can see they are scared of what's going to come next. They are afraid of their futures just like I am. Around 10 in the evening we arrive at my aunt's house.

I remember that the day we arrived at my aunt's house in Tijuana, I felt something inside me that told me, "This is not a good place to live." Ayii, para mi mala suerte, my father told me that I was going to live with my aunt for a couple of months. When I heard that I thought he was joking, but he wasn't.

In that moment I felt he didn't want to take me with them. I felt that he was going to leave me there forever, but that wasn't true, because he had a reason and the reason was that he didn't have enough money para pagar el coyote. But I was blind and I couldn't understand my father, and I asked myself, "Why?" Una y otra vez, and I never got an answer.

Then they left and took my two older brothers and my sister, making me feel like nothing, like I was no longer their son, feeling so lonely I ran to the back yard of my aunt's house. And sitting close to an altar de la Virgen de Guadalupe and I prayed hincado frente a ella. Recuerdo que yo sólo le preguntaba por qué. And I still ask that question, not because of that, but because of the things that are happening to me now.

Living with my aunt was like a nightmare because she was very strict. She was always blaming everything on me. Cuando mis primos hacían una travesura, she would blame me. She never liked me. Ella siempre desquitaba el coraje conmigo.

The only person I could trust was my cousin Mario, mi primo mayor. He was seventeen years old. He was twice as big as me, he was always desatienda con mi tía, defendiéndome de ella. I remember he was always telling my tía, "Madre por Dios no trates así a mi primo. El no tiene la culpa de los problemas entre tu y mi padre—está solo no lo hagas sutor más." But my tía never listened to him. She was too ignorant to understand him.

My cousin Mario, he was the only one who was good to me. I remember that one day he took me to the movies, and my tía got mad because she didn't want me to go out. But my cousin took me a escondidas de mi tía. I remember he liked boxing a lot. In the garage he had boxing gloves and una bolsa para boxear. And he would just go there when he felt frustrated of the problems he had at work and with his mother. When I saw him I felt guilty, I felt I was causing him problems.

One day I was praying for my father to come for me, when I heard a voice saying, ¿"Vámonos te quieres quedar"? —Yo pensé que era sólo en mi mente lo que escuche, then I turned back, and saw my father looking at me with those eyes. Que decían todos los motivos en mis preguntas.

Past & Present

Antonio Avila

I was raised in Fresno, California back in the days when there was not a lot of opportunities for my race. I am not blaming anybody for this, but that was the reality we were living. There was not as much opportunity and advantage as there is now for us.

But the thing that I remember most is no matter what, I had a family. And even though we never had a lot, we still had each other. And that is what has made me and my family not only what we are, but who we are. We are not just Mexican people trying to make it, we are the Avila. But mainly we are a family with a lot of dignity and pride. So I guess when you ask me about my past, the main thing that comes to my mind is my family.

Right now I just have positive things. Trying to graduate, trying to succeed in life. Even though a lot of odds were and are against me, I still have the determination to succeed, not only in high school, but also towards my future and dreams. I know that God set a path for me, but I just need to choose what path I'm going to take, and see if I'm going to follow it. I believe that the path that God has set for me is to graduate, get a promising job, and to be somebody, not only to myself, individually, but to others too.

Sixteen and Older

Sandra Abúndiz

I was sixteen when I got pregnant and seventeen when I had my beautiful little girl which I ended up naming Xiomara Leila Lozano. It wasn't hard for me since I had my mother by my side. She was there for me from the beginning until today. I can't say the same for my father because when I told him that I was pregnant, he reacted just like any normal Dad would react. He kicked me out of his house and told me that the only way I was going to be able to stay there at his house was if I got an abortion, and of course I was totally against it.

So I moved in with my mother because at the time my boyfriend and I were having problems. While I was pregnant, I still kept on working. I even got a second job from a summer job program fixing up gardens and pulling weeds. But in no time did I want anyone to feel sorry for me because I got myself into it and I knew that one way or another I was going to make it, whether if was by myself or with José (my baby's father).

After eight months of being pregnant I was ready to have my daughter, not because it was hard for me, because through my pregnancy, I never did have morning sickness or any of the other things that some women go through. I was ready because I couldn't wait to dress up my little girl with all the things they had given me on my baby shower, which my mom and my two very good friends arranged for me. I always had dreams about my little girl. In my dreams she had a good complexion and blond curly hair with blue eyes, kind of strange since I'm dark complexioned, and I have black hair with brown eyes.

I don't know, maybe I was crazy, but those were the feelings and dreams I had about my soon to be daughter. When I woke up one morning I felt fine, but something wasn't right, so I called José and told him that I was going to have my baby today. He didn't have much to say, but I was happy so it didn't really matter. All that mattered to me was that I had done my part in telling him ahead of time. Now, I just had to concentrate on my baby.

Around ten o'clock that night I left to the hospital with really bad labor pain, nothing unusual for me, since I had my mother by my side to let me know everything that I would be feeling. My mother was real supportive, she was there. My younger sister and only one of my good friends, no one else was there.

I cried, my labor pains were killing me and my whole body hurt and nothing seemed to make it better. Around one o'clock in the morning my little girl was born and exactly the way I had dreamt she would be. Strange, isn't it. Well, not if you're a mother. My baby weighed 7 pounds 15 ounces and she was 21 inches long. She was a real healthy baby, but all I wanted to do was sleep. Everyone came to see her the next day except for her father. But I didn't notice he didn't show up until the following day, and of course, he fell in love with his daughter. He couldn't resist her from then on. Nine months have passed since my daughter was born and nothing could be better. José and I got a little house, moved in together with our little girl, and of course, we stayed in school.

We want to be good role models for our daughter. That way when she grows up she can't rub nothing in our face. José has a part-time job and I stay home taking care of Xiomara. It's been real fun having my daughter and she's made us learn several different things. Being a mother and a father is easy, but if you don't raise and teach your children the morals and the values of life, then you still haven't done your job right.

How I Came To Yakima

Raúl Chacón

My full name is Raúl Chacón Castellanos. I was born in the town of Tepalcatepec Michoacán, México, better known as Tepeque. In my family there are eight persons: my parents, my sister, and five brothers including myself. My parents names are Jesús and Reynalda. My brother's names are José Luis, Juan Manuel, Yesenia, Jesus and Saul Martín.

I had lived in a ranch for about seven years. It was a small ranch called "El Abrebadero." There were like five houses without T.V., lights, just "Aparatos." But in 1986 my family had to move to Colima. It was Cofradía de Juarez, ten minutes away from Tecoman, Colima where I spent my childhood. In Cofradía de Juarez I went to "Ignacio Zaragoza" Middle School, but my first week was a torture for me because I didn't know how to express myself in groups of people. I felt the change from my ranch Abrebadero to Cofradía de Juarez City. I was feeling a rock on my back, I wanted to go back home. I was afraid about people, but I had to "aguantar" because there wasn't another choice. The first week at middle school was a real torture for me. I called it "Fear Days" but finally I overcame this fear. Then I started making friends. Four weeks later everybody knows me very well, but not one of my friends called me by my name, they called me just "Chacón."

Like 5 years later I started attending at "Jesus Gonzalez Lugo" High School at Cofradía de Juarez, Colima México. There I met some of my best friends: Hugo Gomez "El Loco"; Jorge Arreola, "El Perrus"; Oscar Rodriguez, "El Zurdo"; Elias Lopez, la Pucha"; Antonio Cervantes "Tonon", Elias Magallon "El Bronco", Ernesto Lopez " El Neto", Alberto Rosales, "El Chivo", Eugenio Chavez "El Geno", Mario (I don't remember his last name) "El Condorito"; Armando Chavez, "El Mando"; Joel Lozano, "El Borrego"; Alex Padilla, "El Pano"; Aaron Salvatierra, "Aaron"; Israel Eudave, "El Iria"; Martin Paredes, "La Vaca". These are the names and nicknames of some of my friends at "Jesús Gonzalez Lugo High School," Colima México.

In 1993 I graduated from High School, then I started going to the University of Colima in Tecoman, but I went there for about three weeks because my father's Immigration appointment was ready for us at Ciudad Juarez, Chihuahua México. So my family left "Cofradía de Juarez." Our destination was Ciudad Juarez, Chihuahua. There the immigration appointment was consummated. I became a permanent resident of U.S.A. but my parents didn't have too much money to cross the border in to U.S.A. so, we had to come back to Colima again.

One year later I was packing to leave "Cofradía de Juarez" again, but this time a long journey was waiting for me. I had to reach Yakima, WA. It was February 19, 1995 when I left "Cofradía de Juarez" ten minutes later I was taking the city bus in "Tecoman, Colima." I traveled from Tecoman to Tijuana, I arrived to Yakima in the last days of February, 1995.

For the first weeks of March 1995 I came to Davis High School. I still remember my first day of school. I was never confortable for two minutes, so my first class was Drawing with Mr. Kloster. I was lost, and confused. It was like not knowing where you are. I didn't have any idea about what was happening in class, and too afraid to ask some of the Mexican guys for help. But afortunadamente there was a great guy there, he was Rudy Espinoza. He helped me a lot in this class, so I felt a little bit relaxed.

Later I imagined, I didn't ask for help because I was afraid to show my ignorance, yes I was, but not any more. Now three years have already passed, since I left Cofradía de Juarez Colima, México, but I haven't forgotten it. I cannot even know how much time will pass before I could come back to there. So this is how I came to Yakima, but this was not all because, I came from Cofradía de Juarez Colima México looking for new opportunities, and a better life.

Now I am here trying to make a good living because I am the only one with the power to do something about my life, just to be Raúl, or to die being Raúl, it is just my decision, and I don't mean that I have to go see San Pedro but I'll never do something purposely to go see him.

I describe myself as a friendly and peaceful person. I like to watch Soccer and Argentina will be World Champion in France 98 (World Cup). I also like to listen to music, to dance, to write poems and songs, to read the Bible, and have fun whatever I do. One of the most interesting things about me is that I always take a shower. I am a thousand years old, because I never count my age by years, I count it by friends.

My Story

Gabino Salazar

I am Gabino Salazar; I came from a very humble family in Oaxaca, México. If you have the chance, please look at a map for my town which is located southwest of México, look for region of San Juan Mixtepec, and you will find out that the name of the town was given by the Indians of Mixteco.

In September 16, 1979, I was born in region of San Juan Mixtepec. This date sounds pretty good to me because on this date México became independent from the Spaniards and became a wide nation. I think that is why I feel so good with myself every time I see my birth certificate.

At the age of six years old, when I was just starting to understand life and know from where I came from. I could barely remember when my father died. When I was crying that day, my chest was burning. Each time I took a breath, it felt like someone was stabbing me with a knife. I hadn't eaten much of anything for days, so I got weak and sick. When I got sick my mother would have to get loans from friends and take me to the doctor. However, the doctor did not do anything to me, instead, the disease got worse. Then my mother took me to the Curandera. I almost died, but that person returned my life back. After that, we had a lot of loans from people. We could not pay them back, and without my father, it was even harder, and the interest was multiplying every month. There was no job out there to do. We did not have any other choice than to move from one place to another. We went to the North of México looking for a job, for more opportunities and a better life for the family, but, in the winter time, it is very hard to find a job.

We migrated state to state looking for stable jobs,. but it was like anywhere else, there was a lot of discrimination against us, all because we were dark skin.

Finally everybody would have a job and a little more than a year we send money to the person who lent us money, it was a lot but with the help of everybody we completed.

Like three years later in 1990. We got established in Ensenada B. C. Northwest of México in where I started primary school. At the beginning it was very hard, almost impossible, because at that time I did not speak any word in Spanish except Mixteco. Sometimes my friends would call me to play marbles with them. But, I did not understand, what they were saying even with signs was difficult.

One day I was at my aunt's house when her son in-law came and visit her, when the guy got close to me his clothes smelled like tobacco. But, at that moment I did not know that this guy would later send me to the nearest store to get him a packet of cigarettes. I told him that I did not speak any Spanish. Then he told me how to ask for it in Spanish. I headed toward the store repeating the word every step I took, when I got to the cashier, I totally forgot what he told me. I was standing when by coincidence a guy came and bought a package of cigarettes. That made it easier for me to point out the cigarettes. When I got home he ask me why I took so long.

Well, the cashier wasn't there when I arrived. So I had to wait.

Anyway, I flunked my first grade because I did not know Spanish, but the second year I passed all my classes with excellent grades. The principal honored me and gave me a diploma as a student of the year.

There are many reasons why I did not speak Spanish, none in my family could speak Spanish. They all speak Mixteco, actually my mamma understands it a little bit. She could not speak it. My grandmother used to speak Spanish very well. She used to live in Mexico City for about ten to fifteen years. She was afraid to teach my mother because if she learned she could talk to any men that come to sell stuff in the plaza, and would break our tradition.

July 23, 1994 is the date that we first came to the United States of America. My older brother brought us up here because he wanted me to go to school. But I did not know that, I thought we came here to work on the fields. And then he told me to choose between Ike or Davis. I say how can I go to school if I do not speak any English. Those teachers speak only English. Nobody would understand me. He said; that is not my problem you will go to school, tomorrow I will give you a ride to the school and you will register. Call me after school and I will come and pick you up.

I did not have a choice. I went into the office and registered with Mr. Rigney. He told me about classes, then he called a beautiful young girl to guide me to my classes, the first class that we went was ESL, I felt very comfortable there because Mr. Cole could speak Spanish very well. The rest of the periods were teachers with no Spanish at all.

In those periods I had a very hard time because the teachers could not understand me and I could not understand them either. I started to have problems with math lessons, I did not know what to do to get my grades up. But that is in the past.

Now look at me where I am. I am almost to graduate from Davis High School. I will confess to you that I never received any awards or be student of the month from the school I am sad but at the same time I am happy with myself I feel that I had done a great job. I am proud of myself. Because I think I had learned Spanish and English almost well and that makes me feel good.

From now on, I think there is no impossible in our life as long as we want to face it, in a very positive way.

I am grateful to life, to my family to all the people thet surrounded me in my apprenticeship.

For now on I think it is time to fly away for ourselves and face the life as adult people—face the reality of the life.

>I am leaving because I think I am ready to be tested.
>I am leaving because I think I can handle any problem.
>I am leaving because I had won the first part of the Game.
>For those of you who stay please try to win the first part of the game.
>If I made it you also can make it . Like Mr. Rigney says, you are the architect of your life.
>Do not wait to do your homework just do it. Adiós...

I See My World through Your Eyes

Angel Ayon

Poetry is a way for people to express themselves. It is a common way for a person to express the feeling of love. Love comes out in everybody in a different way. We put words together and build them so that they represent us. Love gives us the inspiration we need to get us going. Love is the base of all things. Of how we think, how we live, and how we see one another as equals. Love may have complete control over a person. We tend to follow love wherever it goes and do anything for it.

Words can be so simple, but mean so much. "The birds of night peck at the first stars that flash like my soul when I love you." Like stars, love is forever shining and lasting. When explaining love to somebody, it's difficult because one feels words are inferior to these intense emotions. The strongest way I have seen that can do this for me is using metaphors.

Metaphors give impossible images a way of happening. "Everyday you play with the light of the universe." We see our loves as people who can do the impossible. This person who has captured my heart has enough power to do anything. The image of love I get is a part of me and everything around me. We can be completed with our loves and want them to be a part of us and us a part of them.

We speak through our writings to tell of life's struggles. What we need to do. What we have to do. Loving is loving so many different things. Struggle is in everyday life. I struggle to be a better person each day. I am willing to fight for improvement not only in myself but in my people. The love for each other as human beings and our struggles to get that love is what is most important. As I write I see myself get stronger. I see my love for everything deepen inside of me. My outlook on the little things in life becomes more intense each time.

When I come across love between two people, it makes me step back a moment and look at my own life. I ask myself how I welcome life. I now feel what, where, how, and which ever way I want. Constantly, never letting go of my faith in God. Loving everyone and everything in my way.

I haven't always known this. I am a young woman. When love hit me for the first time I was only 15. I was never really into guys all that much. So when he came into my life, I had no idea what this love thing was. I was overwhelmed by these feelings I had. There was nothing in the world that could pop the bubble this young man and I were engulfed in. My whole being revolved around not me, but us. Years went by and I matured more and more each day. My heart never changed and neither did his. One day without warning, he broke my heart. I was crushed. All that I believed was true seemed to be lies. I was already at the most confusing time in my life. I was trying to find out who I was. I wanted to know what I was all about. Now, I was supposed to know how to <u>live</u> without him. If it wasn't for a very special friend and my parents, I might have turned down the wrong road. But you know what, it wasn't the advice they gave me, or the talks we had, *it was me.* It was just knowing someone else cared for me. It's a hard subject to talk about. To me it was just knowing that if I was to die, I wouldn't be forgotten. That's how strong love hit me. I don't think I can ever forget that period in my life. I still think about him. I wonder how my life would be if I'd never had that mountain to climb. I am grateful because he truly did change my life forever.

It was a time of confusion between right and wrong. Sometimes, with new ways it still is. And that's o.k. To be able to speak this freely about love is a privilege. It is a right given to you when you overcome obstacles. When you are faced with challenges and get through in the end. Not necessarily winning, or losing, but coming out o.k. You have to feel or have felt love to know it and all its powers. Having had mountains in my life to climb has opened my eyes to another world. A world that's filled with passion and a sense of knowing.

Literature explores many ideas—being a person, loving, living, and breaking chains. A person's heart and desires are sometimes put to a test because of family traditions.

In most family traditions, they deal with the woman and it usually suppresses her. Women are being expected to play out the traditional "woman" roles yet portraying them as rompedoras de cadenas. The men see it as a way of respect towards women.

The most common role has the woman being in the kitchen, "being where she belongs." When in fact, here is an example of breaking chains. The woman expresses all of her feeling and turns them into flavors, smells, textures, and effects to the power of food. We are the number one source of power. All the same, the woman has limits put on her. There are boundaries that we must not cross because then we would face discouragement and ridicule that makes us feel powerless. We translate waves around us to realism. To be a woman this is like the sky. Too far to reach. Beautiful and wondrous. We can be horrendous and wild, calm and peaceful.

When we recognize these setbacks we can understand. The men play significantly right into this. Men see how a woman needs more than just cooing and kisses. She needs the intellectual side. She needs to break free from playing the traditional roles. All of her senses must be reached to express inner and true love. Our role as women, is to search for love, and when we find it, to welcome it. So you see we all play roles in life.

We forget about the men sometimes. Often times looking past the roles men play in life. Their roles are just as important as ours. They're strong and mean, yet tender and placid. The men see us and they have an intense longing to want to be part of us. They recognize our feelings and actions. They may not know why or where our energy comes from and that is intriguing and mysterious to them. The roles are being changed drastically between being women, men, and being human beings. No one role or person is better than the other. We all seem to even out and combine smoothly.

Fearfulness in Life: From Omar's Journal

Omar Ramíriz

December 4th, 1997

En Comala pasé los momentos más bellos de mi vida. Pues está localizado a seis kilómetros de Colima, la capital. Comala es conocido como el Pueblo Blanco de América, ya que antes su fachada era completamente blanca. Su famoso ponche y pan, hacen parte de esta bella tradición. Hoy toda la familia fuimos a los portales (son los restaurantes más famosos de la región, en estos restaurantes solo se paga las bebidas todo lo demás es gratis) a celebrar la bienvenida.

I never knew about life until a few years back; when I was growing up in a world filled with anguish between obstacles and beneath my own moon. It was a great fear in my heart, I was not ready to meet the life cycle. My cerebral palsy kept my soul under my blankets. Afraid to meet new people in my world, afraid to open new horizons in my mind.

In late July, I saw the sky triste, glancing at my face. I knew than that it was going to be laborious to continue my destiny. I was not introduced to the roses then, the grief played a major role in my desert garden of love and treason. The hope didn't arrive on time. The blood was detached from my veins, I thought that I was a blunder in life and I worried that my family would think the same way as the ignorant people did. I was about thirteen years old, in a dark life, the brightness didn't exist that dastardly year. I had only three friends I could trust. One of them named Adriana left from my side to México and I only heard one time from her. Since I lost her address, jamás he vuelto a saber de ella. The only thing I know is that Adriana lives in Las Vegas, Nevada.

December 5th, 1997

Cuando se fue todavía estaba cautivado con su mirada y su dulce sonrisa. El sol ha salido de nuevo en mi corazón y la oscuridad se perdió en el abismo, eso pensé porque se me ha abierto un nuevo camino. Con su luz, no me puedo desviar del camino de las espinas amargas porque ella encedió otra vez mi vida. Las rosas van a crecer en el jardín al pie del camino de mi corazón. Te quiero mucho Lupita.

She was the other part of me; she knew the real me inside, my feelings, my dreams, mi tristeza, mi soledad. She didn't care about my physical semblance, la cual a otras personas sí les importaba. Cuando se fue de mi vida, me sentí muy triste because a part of my life vanished with her into the profound ocean. I knew her since third grade in Martin Luther King Elementary school. We were always together, sometimes after school. Era como una hermana para mí, era una gran alegría en mi mundo. In seventh grade, in Washington Middle School, I heard that bitter news, she was leaving and not coming back. When she told me in her tears, I ran like crazy in sorrow and in grief. I couldn't believe her lips, like two rivers breaking apart from the sun.

That day, by her locker getting her things, I walked towards her in tears. —¿Te vas?— I cried. —Sí, me voy.— —¿Cuándo regresas?— —No lo sé, a lo mejor nunca.— She looked down. My tear dropped on the gray floor of the old school (W.M.S.), where some dreams died with her departure. I was speechless, my tears interfered with the voice of the breaks. I didn't know what to say, the two worlds bonded together and the silence took control of the situation. It seemed that I was letting go of my stars, no more jokes, no more laughs, no more hope. She was the other part of me, I felt superior with her because I was normal to her, not like others. Without her I would be lost, trapped in my world again, isolated from the normal human being. —Que te vaya bien,—my last words to her belleza—

in that moment I embraced her and cried as two babies en una cuna. The bitter tears landed on her head y yo lloraba más y más cada momento. Then she followed the steps out into the real world y me quedé llorando con mis ojos rojos, llenos de luto.

December 11th, 1997

We arrived at la catedral de Colima, in search for the forgiveness de nuestra Morena. We were fifteen all together who were seeking the forgiveness. La catedral was filled with peregrinos. I knelt down to my Morena with the rest of my familia to pray. My watery tears slid down my face as a stream in search for the ocean. Her eyes reflected my destiny, the destiny of a real life beneath her heaven of felicidad. Everything was there for me but suddenly the reality came back to real life. Mariachis contributed with us, cantando las canciones para nuestra Virgen Morena. The lloradera came again with us. Mis lágrimas formed into a chain of hope and liberty. In her rostro I saw my life in an abyss but I was safe with my mother, she construes my life again in the atmosphere. A flashback arrived in my river, remembering my father when he was in my ocean. I wished that he was here with us, para compartir esta grande felicidad. Her profile contributed my soul in her world, seeking for the esperanza de la vida. My waterfall continued with the tristeza de a peregrino. We cried, farewell to our Virgen of Guadalupe.

I was craving to arrive in Comala to la parroquia to continue with the ceremony. We heard the mass after the mariachi sang once again to our Madre. It was the twelfth, the special day had arrived in my fruitless eyes. Walking around the jardín de recuerdos bellos, pensando de Lupita la muchacha más hermosa, with the exception of our mother. I will never forget this day, it will be always in my mind like a rose with thorns. Our Morena is an immortal image because she is always with us, en las buenas y en las malas. Without her, the Mexican culture wouldn't exists in our society. She gives esperanza to us, aunque algunos estén lejos de nuestra patria Mexicana. Ella siempre será nuestra Madre de Guadalupe, my heart will always belong to her until the end of my jornada.

<u>*Viva la Virgen de Guadalupe, Nuestra Morena*</u>

The next day in class the teacher took attendance and said her name "Adriana." I glanced at her desk and it was as a desert as my heart. The smile was no longer there, empty chair, no body to warm it up. The hand was not writing anymore on the white paper that was her soul. It came to my mind the song of Pedro Fernández called, "La Mochila Azul." That song explained the whole scene. It wasn't the same, I had to accept her departure forever. During break, I walked to her desk and sat down with pain. I remembered during the break that she and I used to play games or talk about our daily lives. Todo eso, se termino aquél maldito día, cuando se fue. My confidant was gone. Turmoil was added to my life, now I will be apart from everyone. This turmoil was indeed in my mind because I was distinct from the rest, some of them thought that I was a retarded kid who didn't have any feelings, dreams, illusions, or hopes. I accepted that I couldn't do anything about it. It was my essential life-time. It was reality, it was no dream as I had dreamed, only the cursed reality that I dreamed in that night of ice. Accepting my physical condition was difficult, not knowing a real reason for the human spirit.

I only knew Adriana's dream. I couldn't tell my parents, porque no quería verlos sufrir por mi maldita vida. Besides they separated like two rivers as Adriana's lips. Separation of my parents was another topic of the life cycle. My brother Aldo and my sister Jessica were suffering from the restricted earth, too. But everyone in my family is normal, not like me, all retarded, I thank God that it was me, not someone else in my family. Sometimes I think that I am not part of the Ramírez Cruz Family because they live in another dream. They are superior to me, but they have never been ashamed of my prophetic life. I know that Mr. Bodeen, my Latino Literature teacher, hates when I use the word "RETARD," to describe my character. But it's reality, it's not a movie where people appoint their character. As I had said before, life is hard for everyone, especially for me, a retard restricted from love and felicidad, it's irony for me. I only have my roses and my roads that God gave me. A conflict in the universe of cerebral palsy. By the coast, my life had been established and it will never drown in the water.

December 31st, 1997

The last day of the year. Another year that left forever into my heart. Otro año de soledad profunda, otro camino se acabó, hasta aquí llegó su jornada. I had planted seeds in the garden of love, but it had forgotten about me. Each day I get closer to my death. Another year is leaving today, and the felicidad leaving with it. Una vida que no vale nada is staying with la tristeza. The destiny is turning its axes again in my world. Some friends are not here today to celebrate esta derrota conmigo. Another year without the woman you love, un año más en el pasado. Some friends have died, others have vanished from my hands and the rest are far away. December 31st, una gran melancolía en el corazón y alma.

Time had passed, but the turmoil stills exists in my poor mind. My only dream is to leave this world soon as some people had told me. It's true, mi vida no vale nada. Voices haunt me every night saying, "Retard, loser, low life, cursed animal," and more. Again I had to accept those things as my fear. I can't set eyes on anyone because love wasn't born for this cursed retard, que soy. Hardly no one knows the real me inside, they are afraid to speak with me. People have pity towards me. A veces la gente me habla porque me tienen "LASTIMA," I know how that feels. Soy la burla de todos, I am the mockery of everyone. My desire for everyone is that they can know the real me, not the retard that carries a laptop computer during school. It will never happen, pero que bonito es soñar, que todos quieran a uno. My words are what I am. Mi cielo no tiene color, está apartado de lo bueno y vive en un infierno total. El mundo está lleno de hipocrecia e infelicidad. I need to accustom myself to live isolated from people and without a lover. Just pure plain dreams, surrounded by the darkness in which I live in.

The day will come to an end for me, my roads will still continue somewhere in eternity and the roses will keep growing in my family's garden. Life has been always this way, soon a word called, "RETARD" will end. Triumph hopefully will help me comprehend everyone. Seeds in a land of infancy waiting for water to grow. Sardonically the irony will act in a wretched way in time.

January 11th, 1998

Today is our last day in Comala, our voyage had come to an end. We glanced to the plaza for the last time. Los Cadetes de Linares, a famous group of Mexicans and internationals had came to Comala for the first time. This group were the creators of "Una Página Más," and they were in our plaza. I sent greetings to Paty and to my friends. Macho, Aldo, Chelis, and I went there, the rest stayed to pack-up. We sang all the songs, old songs, those are the best. I wanted to squeal because in a few hours, the destiny would leave our past into an abyss. Time was closer and closer. Only I stayed in the plaza after everyone vanished into the salty ocean of desires. This may be my last day here, I may not come back. With tears on the sand of glory, I left a tradition behind the course.

The word "LASTIMA," will quit from human beings sooner or later. The spring will not come without flowers, a tear will not support the soil where we plant seeds of hope. My thorn will cry for a love hidden under the stone. Our hands will cover our desire from earth, a beautiful hand will finish my work. Her face will never reflect a doleful look, a sigh is not sufficient for her beauty. My eyes will close forever and I will never see the nature again. I am sure that no one will care if I leave, they will never notice. To live in this world with an illusion is a crazy hope, to suffer on a heart of thorns. I have to leave everything behind to rest in peace. The fear will last forever like the roads and roses. La vida comienza y al fin se termina, es mejor morir cuando uno no encuentro el amor y la felicidad.

La sala era una melancolía inmensa, Grandpa's hand of gold and honor had the mourning de nuevo. Su cara reflejaba mi tristeza, su rostro lloró cuando me vío. Mi abuela lloró de sientimiento, sus manos estaban calientes y las mis frías. Everyone was weeping, the sympathy was not sufficient. Time arrived. Hugs and kisses were spread among the casa grande. Aunt Bertha cried as a baby, that's why I love the song of "Una Página Más." My grandparents were alone again, their blessings were there for us. I had left two bohemians, two secret lives had to stay to travel the roots of the past. I got on the van of dreams, with a tear in my eye I said,"¡¡¡LOS QUIERO A TODOS!!!" We turned and the lives disappeared on the street. We drove por la calle de medio (main street) and passed by the Church San Miguel Arcángel rezamos antes de partir en nuestra jornada. Two guys were still at the jardín, we honked at them and they yelled, "Que les vaya bien."

Then passed by the last house in el pueblo, with dolefulness we vanished into the darkness. We started the Camino Real and a sign on the road cried, "¡¡¡FELIZ VIAJE!!!""

A Personal Statement

Rafael Villalobos

The following isn't an essay, for the term doesn't exist to me. It's a contribution to myself, and an informing to who shall read it. This shall remind me, and make you remember, the goals of a child, for he is the youngest of four. And how, as well as why, he shall not attempt, but will, achieve them.

For since the first years of his educational learning, he has attended fourteen schools nationwide. From Washington to Florida, of those fourteen schools, only at two has he remained over a year. Proudly, he currently attends Davis High School. There he has taken with him, the knowledge of teachings from across the seas. Each school had motivating people, and that's what has led him to be who he shall become.

•

I see in the experience of my parents, who I cherish and are not with me today, that an education isn't to be taken for granted. Of the two, the highest learning is a third grade education, obtained by my mother. I saw that a man gave life to what he hates, and death to what he feared. This man, my father, believed that knowledge would cause him to change, something a conservative man of innocence should do. For one is innocent until they understand.

I am guilty because I know the truth, and I plan to show my house, which has crumbled, that the foundation built many years ago has not even been chipped, and I shall build anew the greatest history of our name.

By graduating, and going to college.

It all may sound simple, but I already have the graduating part covered. Hard work isn't something that worries me. I find learning the easiest job ever created.

It's much better than waking up at dawn, going to a farm, and spending all day under flames. Working for charity and being able to complain until dusk once the sun has fallen and one is home, agonizing. Only then can one complain, because a good worker doesn't ask questions, nor does he doubt the word of God. A voice that carries over borders to the ears of the desperate, calling them in numbers, in massive groups, so that everyone shall have an occupation. Most to run, and the rest to chase.

And even once we've come, our greatness is but a whisper in a White Republican system of injustice. To them our birth land judges our value. Land we come from, foreign as it is, makes us evil in the eyes of the majority.

I don't like to explain, but get others to question. Once they have, I support them. You see...my dream is to help, build, and conquer. To give a hand, to receive gratitude, to construct truths so that others may see, understand, and banish that which detains an individual from being all he can be. I'm not the army, but I'm prepared to fight a war. As a poet, student, son, as a man of diversity, and a child of hope. My war is everywhere, and for everyone, and to see my mother cry in joy.

When I First Decided to Come To the United States

Angel Gonzalez

This is my first story about my life. I first decided to come to the United States when I was eleven years old. At that time, I was living with my grandma because my parents were here in California working and making money to come back to México. My parents returned to Zacatecas to visit us. They had been in California living for a long time and hadn't come to visit us. They had lived in the United States since 1987. When they returned to México, and I saw my parents for the first time, I was so happy because it was the first time I had seen them since they left me when I was six years old, and living with my grandma.

Cuando de primera mira mis padres estaban contentos, mi madre me abrazó y me dio un beso en la mejilla. Then I remember she asked me how I was. I told her I was all right. Then the day passed and my parents had to return to California. They had only come to México for a couple of days because they left my sister with mi tía. My mom would worry about them. She and my father had asked me if I wanted to come with them, or if I wanted to stay with my grandma. I said, "YES!" I was so happy. They said that if it was all right, I needed to pack up all of my clothes and be ready for the next day to leave.

It was on Saturday afternoon when we left. When we were ready, mis padres se estaban despidiendo de mis abuelos. Porque ya íbamos a salir yo también fui a despedirme de mis primos y amigos. Recuerdo cuando me despedí de mi abuela ella me dio su bendición. She started crying because we were leaving her. Then we left about 11:00 in the morning. We took the bus to Tijuana. When we arrived in Tijuana around 6:00 in the afternoon. I was the only one that didn't have any papers. My father gave me pasara a este lado. Mi padre came with the coyote. He told him it was easy to cross on this side of the border. My father told him where they'll be waiting for me, and they will pay him the money. When we crossed the border, we were so happy, because it is great to be on this side. My parents were already waiting for me in the place where he told the coyote to leave me. We then went to the bus station to take the bus to California. They bought three tickets to come. The bus left and we sat on the bus, estaba ancioso.

La Ilusión

Martha Ponce

A veces uno escucha tantas cosas de las personas que van de Estados Unidos a México, que despiertan gran curiosidad a las gentes que escuchan todas estas cosas que siempre son bonitas, como por ejemplo; que acá hay mucho trabajo, que pagan bien, que te puedes comprar el carro que quieras, en fin tantas cosas, que la gente que no conoce la realidad se ilusiona y surge en ellos el deseo de venir a esta tierra maravillosa que los está esperando con mucho trabajo y dinero, que les va a poder ayudar para darles una mejor vida a sus hijos y esposa.

Y emprenden la aventura algunas piden prestado y si tienen algunos pertenencias las venden para conseguir el dinero para venir a este país. Pero la realidad, la empiezan a conocer, precisamente en el principio de la aventura. Cuando llegan a la línea que divide estos dos países se empiezan andar cuenta que no somos bienvenidos si entramos por la puerta principal y que mucho menos nos van a dejar trabajar y vivir como nosotros pensábamos y son cosas que desgraciadamente las personas que van a presumir a estas, personas, no les dicen la verdad, y los dejan que se hagan falsas ilusiones.

Y lo más triste es que algunas, ni pasan ni regresan, o si regresan, regresan en una caja de madera ya para ser sepultados. Como mi amigo Rafa. Era un hombre ya adulto, casado ya con tres niños. Alguien le contó de EEUU y se ilusionó. Tenía un puesto en el mercardo de la colonia donde vivíamos, pero él quería tener más y darle mejor vida a su esposa y sus hijos. El consiguió el dinero para venirse. Se vino junto con un señor que también vendía en el mercado. Eran buenos amigos. Rafa traía buen dinero incluso el le prestó dinero a su amigo para venirse. Pero ninguno de los dos pudo pasar y sólo uno regresó. Nadie sabe en realidad qué fue lo que pasó o cómo pasó; pero Rafa no regresa con vida. Su amigo dice que sufrio un ataque cardíaco por tanto esfuerzo al tratar de escapar de la migra

Pero hay algunos que dicen murmuran que él fue quien le ocasionó la muerte para quitarle su dinero. Y hay otros Ramírez. La verdad es que solo Dios sabe que pasó.

Y lo triste es que así como éste....triste caso. A diario pasan en las diferentes fronteras cosas parecidas ya que cada vez es más la gente que por las gran necesidad que hay en nuestros países, emprenen esta triste y arriesgada aventura, dejando familias y las pocas pertenencias que tengan y no saben si algún día las volverán a ver.

II. Interviews with Our Mothers & Fathers

At 40 years of age, mom feels like a braveheart
que puede luchar against all the obstacles
that life brings.

Cesar Vaquera

My Mom's Interview

Cesar Vaquera

Let me take you back into time en un pueblito llamado
Antonio Amaro en el estado de Durango México. The year 1955.
A little girl was born just like every child that's born into this world.
Her name, Oralia Perez Martinez.
She is the second oldest of eleven children.
Mi abuelita Raquel Martinez Sosa was married at sixteen years of age and in the same pueblo. It's funny to know that every two years she had a child, until she had eleven children. José Luis, Maria Oralia, Blanca Neli, José Felix, Raquel, José de Jesus, Maria Cristina, Hector, Norma, Rebeca, y el más joven de todos, José Manuel, asi es el orden de nacimientos.

School was always something Oralia enjoyed even though she would separate herself from all the other kids due to her insecurity. You see, they didn't have much. She wore rags and ran around bare footed through the rocky mud slides the rain would cause. Her parents were very poor and could only afford one meal per day. There weren't any cookies, or candies, in her house or in her mouth. The schools didn't even serve breakfast for the early birds and when lunch came around it wasn't there. She was a little sporty as a matter of fact. She was an all-star champion in volleyball.

My mom remembers studying math and all the other subjects. But never once did she get the attention she needed, due again to the low income and her second hand clothes. Her teacher would use her to do her house chores like washing the dishes, laundry, sweeping, mopping, and baby sitting her child during school. She didn't do it for money cause they didn't give her any only once a piece of cake. Being a kid, that's all it took to say she did a good job. This all happened in the third and fourth grade y mi abuelita ni se dio cuenta de esta situación. She'd go home and climb the trees to entertain herself at home. Hasta que su tía Lupe de Pacoima California le mandó una muñeca que tenía ojos y pelo como ella. Lupe had also given her clothes to wear for misa y para la escuela.

My mom was told never to play with her doll outside of the casa, porque de seguro las otras niñas se la quitarían. Well little did she listen, stepping outside into the thin air of jealousy standing upon her was a much taller girl. Margarita, aka Magga, was fourteen and seven years older than my mom. She looked at my mom with a friendly smile, asking to see her doll. She slowly reached out with the doll in hand and like a baby she was careful not to drop it. Oh yeah she thought she had a friend. Magga como una gata le estiró las patas, los brazos and that was only after she poked the dolls eyes and pulled all her hair. The little girl with the only doll who had hair stood in tears after it was thrown in pieces to the floor like a puzzle. She picked her shattered baby, at least what was left, the hair, legs, arms, head and the body piece that attached every bit of it showing her mom in upset. Mi abuelita didn't punish her. I mean what punishment could you possibly give to a little girl who seemed to have nothing to cherish but a doll and a scar in her memory.

It took years of maturity to forget about the doll. Life went on in Antonio Amaro but now, young and beautiful and attracted to un niño del pueblo. Oh yeah, some young kid had the hots for my mom. His name was Gabriel Rios curly hair, green eyes and light skin almost güero, como el gringo. She dated him at the age of 15 for at least about a year because he moved out and it was a sure thing he changed. My mom heard rumors about him like the ones we deal with today, she said. My mom was heart broken and had pure friends amigos y amigas. There were no relationships for six months straight. Dance was always a part of her life folklórico el baile de los Mexicanos.

She wore dresses so bright they reflected the sun rays. She danced so good, so hard with joy, happiness, and with all the love in her heart, you could feel it in the air's gusting wind. So many years passed without a love in her life. Just friends, always friends. Until she met a guy who was interested in her but later to find out he was violent. So she called it off in one month. Oh yeah, and he wasn't going to let her slip away but he had no choice he had to change his act or move on. My mom later received a letter she never read or touched because her mom hid it from her for a whole year. He had written he changed, and wanted her to go live with him en la ciudad Clarita, pero mi abuelita didn't want her to get involved. I guess they had a bad encounter and didn't want her daughter to fall into a web of lies.

My Mother's journey went on, and being one of the oldest she'd put her little sisters in check because they were lazy, and never picked fights with her brothers. She then remembered all the chores she'd done for what was then coming home, hearing un señor saying: "Look at my daughter in-law". That guy was "kraze" she thought as she kept walking to her grandma's house cuzz she had to set up for her family's reunion. The time came for celebration, fiesta, yeah, everyone arrived. People she knew and some that she didn't know. Everybody said their hello's from hugs, kisses, handshakes, and even the dog was giving handshakes. Mi amá lo quería saludar y el perro le dio la pata izquierda, when it usually picks up his right pata. Well I guess the dog was fed up with all the people and all the handshakes he'd given, so he bit my mom in the leg. Kraze dog got away with it too and lived to be an old dog and later to die on his own, to live the afterlife in doggy heaven. But like all wounds it healed.

She had a friend named Rosia ella a estaba con un joven en la capital de Durango. He drove a motorcycle and every other weekend she'd come to Antonio Amaro para visitar. Well you see she already was with someone else from the town but she thought he was gone. Well little did she know he stood there watching as she arrived with this motorcycle freak. This guy was smart my mother mentioned and never flunked a grade. His name, José Vaquera Marquez, the little boy, son of that kraze man who would always say, "Look at my daughter in law." I guess my mom had a crush on him since childhood but was too shy and she thought he wasn't interested. Two weeks passed and Sundays, always a nice day for a baile. My mom and her friend went, and so did José y sus amigos. It was kraze. José asked my mom to dance and they never sat down or took a break as they danced the night away. Her friend Rosia was jealous and still had feelings for him but it was her own fault. The night was over, everyone went home including my mom. One week later José invited her to a bautismo and the words of his older brother were, "Man if you let her go there must be something wrong with you." So they danced a couple of songs, then later they sat down to talk. He said words she thought he'd never say. —Como te quiero.— My mom didn't know what to say. He put her in the spot by saying, "Do you want to be with me?" "Give me three days to think," my mother replied. "You either say yes now or say no and I'll never bother you again." He was serious and my mom saw that in him. They dated four months.

Mi ama estaba en el Paso, Texas working and taking care of some children that weren't her own. Mientras José su padre y un hermano fueron a cruzar el Rio Grande to visit her in El paso. Mi ama pensando que él le llamo a una de sus hermanas y le comunicó diciendo no se encuentra. Well lejos de aquí cerca de allá José, el padre y el hermano nunca llegaron porque la cruzada estaba muy difícil. José came back from his journey looking for love. I mean he had it but he didn't get to it.

My mom went back to el pueblo. She missed everyone she loved, family, friends, and all in four months that felt like she was imprisoned from her dreams. Ella vio a su tío Jesús Martinez el unico hermano de mi abuelita. She asked to make a call to Piedras Negras en Coahuila México. He let her make the long distance call. Ringggg, Ringggg, una voz diciendo alo— Bueno esta Joséillo Vaquera, Dime con quien hablo? Soy yo, Oralia, I heard you were looking for me. Porque? Oralia es que deveras me quieres? "Sí te quiero y quería oír tu voz."

Ocho meses de novios se pasaron. She always wanted a family you know, kids, but before all that she dreamed of the man she loved. Vestida de blanco. Bueno los padres de mi ama, presente a su lado el sacerdote local en el año del 73, 12:00 p.m. The next day early, six in the morn, preparations for the wedding had started. My mom was nervous but ready to walk the aisle. Till death will she part from his side, and she hoped with the same feelings for him. Everything was great in her life. She had her first born in July 28,1975 my sister Violeta Perez Vaquera.

A second child, this time a little boy. She named him Miguel Angel Perez Vaquera. He's 21 years old now going to Alaska on the 7th day of January, leaving to work on a fishing boat. I wish him luck.

When my mom was pregnant with me she was having problems in her marriage. My padre, or so called father that I had was cheating. It was an unforgettable memory and journey. I mean the whole situation, coming to the land of opportunities and with me in her womb, including two young ones, to take care of, it even made it more difficult. She finally made her destiny for us all and without the man she loved. We lived in an apartamento en los Angeles, City of Angels. She had to work really hard at a warehouse full of bad air, loud noises, and having to walk five blocks away from city boundaries with me. It was kraze cause the money wasn't enough then, and isn't enough today, as I tell the story of my mother. January is welcoming the New Year and on the third day I wasn't out. Yes I was third in line to be born. I looked like a monkey, a little changito. She didn't want me but she had no choice because she felt there was something special about me.

Well her story doesn't just stop there, you see my mother had moved on with her vida. Yes she had feelings for him, but never will she take him back. As the years, mornings, nights, passed, she moved to the Evergreen State. I guess there was money to be made in the fields near a city called Yakima. A place where she got a small apartment full of cuca-rachas. She wanted the best for us because we were all she lived for. She met an older man someone who is now taking the place of my father. You know the guy who was not taking care of his. Why'd he do it! My mom doesn't even know. Elias B. Rodriguez was a preacher man spreading the word, la palabra de Dios. When and how she met him, I sometimes ask myself. I speak for my brother and sister who I heard cry. I was in the mix also, getting hit by a leather belt. What life brought into our world was a living hell. Many kids at school wondered why our hair wouldn't grow more than an inch. You know he had this thing for clippers. You know what, we were abused and I can't believe we made it this far. Tears and cries are something I'll always remember from the ones that fell out of my eyes, to the ones that didn't and to the ones I can't hear. My father is the one above, no matter what words of my mother that I'll cherish forever. I knew life wasn't going to be easy and it never will.

My childhood years is something I dislike due to the abuse, but within time things started to change. I had to look for a father figure in the streets of this city. I ran through the barrios and found ways to take the pain and memories away. I used drugs, alcohol, hard liquor, I used to guzzle that bottle like an infant. I thought I was invincible. Nothing could take me down cuzz the demons in my head were so high off marijuana and I couldn't sleep—the cocaine cutting my nostrils wouldn't let my mind rest. You wonder my estilo today and what I'll be tomorrow. You see you'll never know if I'm living in earth, heaven or hell. This isn't just some simple assignment to turn in and hand in. This is reliving the past, I don't like it, neither do I hate it. I don't blame anyone for what has happened because I'm living today drug free. Everyone in this life has a mirror and they can see many things in it. I see love, hate, sex, violence, crime, art, life, pain, and everything the blind eye can't see. But deep within the roots of my todays, I pray and thank our Father above for helping me survive all life, from the system, to its courts, y cada consejo that I listened to, especially my mother's. Everything I see is good even when it's really bad.

1998. I'm nineteen I'm involved in life in every which way. And well it doesn't matter where I'm going or where I'll be tomorrow or in my later years. I know I can survive anything that's in my way. I can forgive and forget. I can do anything I want, be anything and have anything. As I write, I'm wishing and praying the same for you. We're more than conquistadores. You know! Even better when left alone.

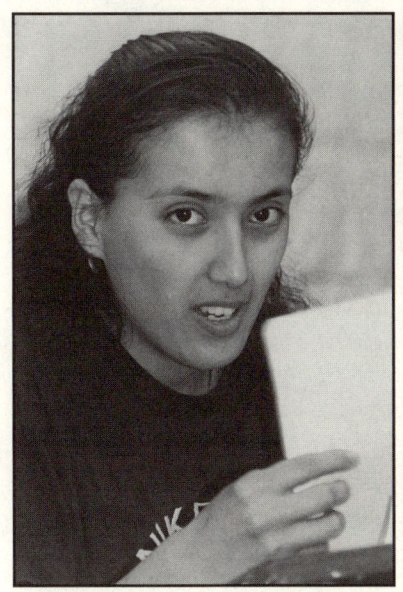 

Two Sisters Write About Their Mother

Maira Cárdenas and Adriana Cárdenas

My mother Martha Avalos de Cárdenas was born on September 3, 1955 in a small rancho in Michoacán called El Paso de Arriero. She lived there for six years and then her family moved to San Miguel Colima, a small Ranchito.

At the age of four, my mom would spend most of her time swimming in a river that ran near her house. She tells me that if she would have spent more time in the water se iba a convertir en Sirena. She also liked to climb trees arrancar guamuchiles y anonas maduras (some kind of fruit) but once climbing a tree de ciruela, she slipped and got her dress caught. She had to wait a long time till someone saw her and helped her down.

I asked my mom what kind of toys she used to have. She laughed as she remembered y me dijo: "The only real toys she had were canicas." (marbles). Her dolls were made out of olotes crossed together and tied. Their clothes were old rags, los carritos eran hechos de basijas. But, my mom says that she would never be bored, always had fun.

Unlike school she wasn't very good. Actually my mom wasn't really interested. Mi mami duró 3 años en primero, 2 años en segundo grado y 3 años en tercero. I asked my mom if she skipped or anything to repeat grades so many times. With a smile in her face she said "no, yo iba todos los días porque era donde se juntaban todos los niños y donde tenían juguetes." Mi mami recibió hasta el tercero grado de educación porque hasta ese grado daban classes en el rancho. There were other schools out of town, but it was too far and too expensive.

When she went back to Michoacán para visitar a su bella (that's what she called her grandma). Mi mami se acuerda que su Bella siempre tenía una imagen de La Virgen de Talpa rodeada de flores y también tenía un frasquito lleno de chicles de Talpa. Y como mi mami era bien traviesa, cuando su Bella no estaba mirando le agarraba los chicles uno por uno hasta que no quedaba ninguno.

At the age of fourteen my mom had some responsibilities, but not too much because almost all were taken by her older sisters. Hers were taking care of younger siblings, going to get water del pozo, and from time to time milk cows.

Still the same age, my mom had her first boyfriend who she didn't have permission to have, but it was all right because her older brothers wouldn't threaten him.

When my mom was 16 she met my dad who was a visitor to the rancho from Tecoman. They started going out, sneaking from my mom's parents, but their hiding wasn't very good. My abuelito caught them and almost hit my dad with a machete. After the scare my dad finally talked to my abuelito to get permission. Several months passed and the age of 17 my mom got married. After the wedding my mom went with my dad to live con los suegros. My mom had some problems con su suegra y las cuñadas porque según my mom married up and my dad married down. So after about 3 months they moved to Guadalajara. It was hard for them, there with their jobs barely giving them enough para comer. So they only stayed there for six months.

Decidieron venirse al norte. The plan was to come for a while to work then head back home soon and with some cash in their pockets. They knew it wouldn't be easy and that they would have to work hard in the fields and they also knew that it wouldn't be easy to get to the other side, but they were willing to take the risks and work the hard labor.

In February of 1974 my mom, my dad and their four month old son, pasaron al otro lado. Walking all night, ducking from light, holding their breath, afraid to breathe as any car or anything that moved would pass by them. They weren't able to eat or rest and while jumping fences. They took turns calling my brother. My mom says she was tired and scared. There was times she thought she would never make it.

They then lived in Pasco, someone lent them a house to live in and my mom got her first job in the U.S. podando uvas. They also lived there for one month porque la migra estaba dura. Then her, my dad, and my brother, Jaime, came down to Yakima, but only for 3 weeks, then down to L.A. then to Chicago for a year and a half. My mom got pregnant there with Concha, but neither my dad, nor my mom wanted to have her born in the U.S. They figured there was no point for that since they would only be here for a little time. So they returned to Tecoman where Concha was born. But their stay in México didn't last long and after six months she was back in Chicago, but now with two kids to take across the border. Two kids to send to the baby-sitters while my mom and dad worked. They spent three years there and then moved to L.A., but now with four kids. Jaime, Concha, Reina y Adriana. The stay in L.A. wasn't for long because after one year they all came to Yakima with another little girl. Here in Yakima they had Ramón, Ismael and Victoria. There they started working, picking cherries, peaches, strawberries. pears, hops, etc.

My mom tells me that it was hard for her to keep moving over and over again. Always looking for work and a place to stay. Starting over and over again. Now working very hard they were able to raise their family and at a very early age we all helped them in the fields.

I also asked my mom "What were your dreams as a child? What is it that you always wanted?" She first answered. "You should be very happy of what you have." She adds, a child always dreamed of having a pair of shoes, not just guaraches. Guaraches that's all she ever had. She also told me that her family really appreciated when they got a new shirt or pants. They wore it to church on Sunday or special places, so they wouldn't wear out as fast.

I also asked my mom, "Do you still want to go live in México?" She got sad and paused for a while then said "No, ya para que voy solo para llevarle flores a mis padres." I got kind of depressed and started to think of how hard it is for her to go back and see her Rancho. The empty house made from branches. She remembers the burro my abuelito had that always went with him everywhere. I looked at her, gave her a hug and said thanks.

Now at the age of 42, my mom is a very strong woman who has gone through a lot of hard situations and always managed to come out of them with a smile and a laugh. She is a woman a mother and a fighter.

From A Small Town Called "Xaloctoc"

Teresa Roque

Maria Alvarez was born in a small town called Xaloctoc, Guerrero on September 17, 1956 to Martín and Victoria. When she was small her mother, Victoria, died.

"I don't remember my mother at all," she replays, There were five girls in her family. Their father left when she was small. They lived with their grandparents Eduardo and Paula. Maria had a hard life, when young. Her sister and she had to get up very early about 4 o' clock in the morning. They had to clean the kitchen, milk the cows etc… then go to the mill to get the maíz for the tortillas. While one did the tortillas, the other did the breakfast. Afterwards they had to go to the fields. One would stay home and do the lunch to take to the fields. Maria always got to take the food to her grandfather and she had to walk about 2 miles since their grandfather had lands far away from home.

"My life was hard since I had no mother. My grandmother was a mother to me, but not enough how I wanted her to be. My grandparents had little money to sustain us. Sometimes they had only enough money just to go to the mill and we only ate tortillas with salt. She took good care of her clothes since she had only some pairs of clothes. When she went to school, she went without shoes, just barefoot. She remembers when she had to salute the flag they made her grandfather buy her shoes, because it was inappropriate for marching without shoes. Her first new pair of shoes made her very happy. She didn't wear the shoes to school, in fact she had them kept in a shoe box. She took them out when she got to march and when it was over, she took them off and put them back in the shoe box.

Times went, happy, sad and crazy times, but then she met her husband to be Alejandro Díaz. They met when she went to get water. Some few days passed and suddenly he asked Maria to marry him, and her answer was yes. She recalls, "When I got to your father's family I was shy, because they had different customs than I did." She got to a rough start, they made bad comments behind her back because she came from a poor family and without parents, they considered themselves wealthy because they had enough money to buy groceries or anything else they needed every week or so. She lived a rough time with that family and they treated her like dirt, even though she did everything by herself, the house work and work that was suited for men.

When her first son Juan was born they improved the way they looked at her, then came a baby girl named Teresa. One day Maria received a letter from Alejandro, and he was in the United States telling her that he wanted his children and her to come to the United States. She decided right away to leave, but things got complicated. She could only take one child with her, it was really hard for her just to take one child. She decided only to take the baby girl, she remembers how hard was it for her that she has no mother at all. She ended up in Yakima, Washington. She didn't have to struggle too much, Alejandro already had a good job and an apartment. She started working in the fields, the same place where Alejandro worked. They worried about their son left in México, and the immigration for they had no papers to be in the United States. She recalls, "One time we had to run away from immigration and we hid in an apple orchard."

Months passed and they heard they could get their papers by applying. They finally got the papers that told them they could stay in the United States for good. As soon as they got their papers they decided to go and see their son, but things didn't go right. They had to stay, because they had some problems. Years past and they had another child, a boy named Alejandro Jr., and then José. Some months passed and then they decided it was time to go to México and see their son. Now every year they make that visit, still living in the same apartment for 16 years and Maria now in her 40's. She had a baby girl and they both decided that it was time to buy a house, since now the whole family was together. They bought a very nice house, and now she tends to forget about the worst things that happened in her life, she only thinks about the future.

Interview With My Mother

Ricardo Acevedo

Maria De Jesus Acevedo.

My mother is very beautiful. She has long brown hair, green eyes, light skin and a great smile. She likes to wear light colored clothes, not too flashy. She loves the dark, single green color. She likes colors that don't cause too much attention. She has a lot of sweaters. She doesn't like to wear too much jewelry. She only wears one or two rings and a necklace her mother gave her. She works a lot. After coming home from work she cooks dinner for the family and cleans the house. She is a very loving mother and takes good care of me and my brothers and sisters. My mother was born on April 21, 1946.

My mother was born in El Salitre de Copala, Michoacán. She was raised in a Rancho far away from the city. There really wasn't much for her to do as a little girl. She would play with rag dolls my grandmother Sofia made for her. She would also make little plates and cups out of clay for my mom to play with. My mom was really full of mischief as a little girl. She would always get into something and would end up getting in trouble.

She told me about this one time my grandpa (Ramón) was gonna go out to the mountain and look for the cows. My mom wanted to go and kept asking and asking but every time my grandpa said no. My mom was really mad and wanted to go really bad, so she left without anyone seeing her. My grandpa was still inside the house and didn't even notice. My mom walked through the path and cut through the woods. At about half way down the path, my mom hid behind some bushes and waited for my grandpa to pass by. She was there for several minutes when my grandpa shows up on his horse. She came out and my grandpa was mad yet surprised to see she had gotten there. He didn't want to take her but had no other alternative. He put my mom on the horse and took her with him.

My mom now lived in Jipimo, Michoacán. She would do all the chores around the house. Also, my grandpa Ramon, sent my mom down to a man named Rafael Gutierrez so he could teach her how to make pants and other clothes.

My mom met my dad at this age, it was all because of this man named Rafael Mendoza. He told my dad (Raúl) about my mom. My dad got interested and rode his horse four hours to the town where my mom lived. My dad just passed by and seen her hanging the laundry. The next day my dad returned and talked to my grandpa (Ramon). He asked him if he could talk to my mom and my grandpa let him. That same day my dad went up to my mom and asked her if she wanted to be his girl friend. My mom told him that she would think about it because she didn't even know him. My dad said that he would return soon, and left. My dad returned one week later because he lived really far. They really didn't talk, because my grandpa would be right next to them so my dad would give my mom a letter and would leave and return two or three hours later. Then my mom would have a letter waiting for him. The relation went on like this for a long time.

My mom had now been married for ten years. She was thirty years old. She had six kids, from oldest to youngest were: Jesús Alvarez, Sandra Elizabeth, Evelia, Carlos, Hugo y Raul. My mom worked in a big clothing factory sewing clothes. They were living in San Valley, Cal. at the time, but soon left back to México because my grandpa was really sick. When they arrived my dad bought a little store. It was a little super market type store and my mom had to run it by herself. It was really hard for her because she had to take care of Raúl and Carlos, and Hugo at the same time. The only day she would have a little fun and some time off was on Sunday. The whole family would go to El Jardín and sometimes would go to the rodeo. That was also the day she would go visit my grandpa because he was ill.

At the age of forty, my mother now lived in Yakima. She was working in an apple orchard hiding her pregnancy. When she would get out of the car to go and pick apples, she would already have her picking bag on and a really loose sweater so they couldn't tell she was pregnant. She stopped picking on Oct. 27. About one month later on Nov. 24 my little brother, and last brother, was born. My dad didn't go to work that day, because he had been up all night at the hospital with my mom. He called the boss and told him what happened. He didn't believe my dad, because my mom had been working there a month ago and he didn't notice her being pregnant. The next day he asked some of the other workers and they told him it was true. He was really mad at himself for not noticing, she could have been hurt.

My mother changed a lot when she got married on April 11, 1966. After being married she felt a greater responsibility for everything, her home and for herself. When she lived with her parents she didn't have to worry about having food on the table or have to worry about clothes. Her parents were the ones with the responsibility. Now that she was married she had to get up really early in the morning and make lunch for my dad and all the helpers he had. She would have to milk the cows and make cheese to sell and also she would make clothes to sell.

When I asked my mother what her dreams were she told me she didn't have any. I told her "Come on mom, everybody has dreams."

"When you live under strict orders and you're always being told what to do, you don't have time to dream. Why get caught up in something that you know is not possible and won't come true? Everything that I have done or accomplished is because God wanted it to happen that way, not because I planned it or wished for it," she said to me.

The life my mom had in her rancho was like a routine life. It was an everyday thing. She had to get up really early in the morning and make my dad his lunch. Then she would milk the cows to make cheese to sell. My mom would sell cheese to the neighbors and my grandpa (Ramon) sells it in town. She has to do all the chores around the house, feed the animals, and go to the river and wash the clothes. She would always be very busy.

My dad used to come down to the United States every year and work in the apples and hops. My mom was left all alone with the kids and she felt too much responsibility and felt that the kids needed to be with their father and decided to come down. Also they were looking for better opportunities and a better life.

Background

Juan Romo

Teresa Ramos' family had many wonderful stories to tell. Some were mind-puzzling and others were just plain scary. It started with Andres Arzaga, son of one of the wealthiest families in Chihuahua, Chihuahua México. At this time, Eusebia, (Teresa's mother), one of the prettiest ladies in the little town, fell in love with Andres, and Andres felt the same way, but his parents opposed them because they didn't want their son to marry a *campesina*.

Time transpired and in the end they were married and then came Teresa, the oldest of the five sisters. The most important of the historical items in the life of Teresa was their house which holds many secrets which will remain a mystery to this day. The house was located on the avenue which carried the name 20 de Noviembre, and this was a house of true historical content to Teresa. It was there that her Great Grandmother was assassinated on those very steps of her house. She was stabbed to death when one of the daughters of her Great

Grandmother left a man for another man. Her Great Grandmother had told her daughter to leave this man. And the man seeking relations went to her house, knocked on the door, and stabbed her four times in the heart, killing her. This house is also historical because in this particular house, spirits roam because they have unfinished business to take care of that didn't get worked out during their lifetime. This house is also important to Teresa because in those thick adobe walls lies a great treasure left by Andres' father before he died.

Maria Teresa Romo

Maria Teresa Romo was born in México's largest state, the state of Chihuahua. In a city named Chihuahua, also. She was born February 6, 1951. She was born to Andres Arzaga and Eusebia Rodriguez. Teresa was a woman that had struggles ever since she was a young lady. She referred to herself and not having a childhood because ever since she could remember, which was at age of eleven, because her tired mind and soul impeded her to remember any earlier. She could remember having to wake up at four in the morning every day and doing duties of a full grown woman.

She always said her childhood was hard, like I started in the last paragraph. She would wake up at four O' clock in the morning and put the coffee in the pot and heat it, then her mother would make her walk a distance equivalent to that of about three miles every morning. During that walk she would pick up corn from the mill to make the tortillas. In the morning she had to make sure all of the kids were showered and dressed for school, (those who went, because her parents couldn't afford to pay for all the children). Teresa had to go to school in the afternoon because her whole morning was spent inside the house doing the chores before she went to school. Teresa also remembered constant harassment from her schoolmates because her parents were not financially stable, they couldn't afford new clothes for her. Her clothes were made from any kind of fabric that could be found and she remembered interval struggles having to cope with this harassment. Teresa never had a chance to act her age because her mother impeded her. Her mother was a very demanding woman, and therefore she had to obey or else she could expect a whoopin' from her mother.

Teresa had the greatest of respects towards her mother even if she disagreed with her mother's points of view. She would never say anything, because to Teresa, her mother was everything. As a young girl she told me that one of her dreams was that when she had her own kids her kids wouldn't live the life that she did. Teresa's struggles continued. There was a time in Teresa's family that they didn't even have money to afford any food so then Teresa's education went out the window, she was forced to find a job to help her family out. She found several jobs as a maid in several different houses around Chihuahua. The thing she remembered was that at these houses she actually felt like a human being because even though she had to clean for a living, she would get treated like a true human. She said that her bosses actually had considerations for her. Teresa's internal struggles continued due to that fact that she wasn't getting any education. It really ate away at her, day in and day out she would cry because she really had a love for knowledge, but she was unable to receive it.

Teresa grew up and the need for income grew greater because her sisters began to get pregnant and that meant that there were more mouths to feed. Teresa and Dolores, the second oldest of the sisters, decided that they both had to work to support the family. Teresa's mother had received some livestock in exchange for a job that Andres had done and she began to breed pigs for market and just in case it was needed for food, for the family. Things went all right for some time. Teresa and Dolores worked along with the selling of the livestock. They made a little bit of extra income. At this time my mother told me of the time that her mother became ill. Her mother had gotten to the point that she had somewhere close to about eighty pigs, but there was one pig in particular that her mother was real proud of, the stud. One night while the family was asleep somebody came and stole her biggest pig. My grandmother, infuriated, became very ill due to this upsetting event and she was never the same. Her mother came down with a series of illnesses and the greatest of them was diabetes. After being diagnosed with this disease things had to change because due to the illness, medication had to be bought to control her blood pressure. She became very irritable and she was always sick. Teresa, at the sight of this was, forced to work a couple of more jobs to be able to support the family and buy medications for her mother.

The family was growing up so then a couple of her brothers had to start working to help support the family because Teresa and her sisters couldn't do it all by themselves. My mother at the sight of this decided she couldn't take it any more.

She left Chihuahua in hopes to find a better paying job. At the age of twenty three she had her first kid, Alfredo Romo. This ordeal, in itself was another struggle because in these times to have a kid and not being married was an embarrassment to the family. And to her was shameful. Now, having a mouth of her own to feed, she felt the urgency to find a job because things were looking bleak for her and her newborn baby boy. She struggled for weeks trying to find a job until one day she got the crazy idea to try and get a job where the offices at the border were located. Here they handled all the affairs of exportation and importation of goods and stuff like that . When she tried to apply for a job they asked her if she had any education worthy of recognizing. My mother's answer was that she had received a sixth grade education and she was turned down for the job. She distinctly remembers going home and crying because it wasn't her fault that she couldn't get an education. That was all she had wanted all her life but her parents were unable to provide it for her. She kept on bothering the people at the offices. She went and went and went, and she was turned down every time until one day she must have gotten the secretary tired of her and she decided to give her an entry level secretarial position.

My mother was filled with joy. This job served as another way of getting an education because here she learned to read at a higher level and she learned to work with people, and she learned valuable skills, like typing, and she worked her way up to the point that she became one of the two head accountants of the office. Things were on the side for Teresa. During these eight years that she lasted working at this office, seven of them went really good, because she was making money by the bundles. During this time she had money to buy everybody new clothes. She bought her mother all of her medications, she bought her dad several trucks, but she forgot to invest in herself. During this period of time she sustained two families on her own and her mother's.

Then there came a time that México went through times of devaluation of the peso. Teresa was devastated by these times because her money no longer bought all the things it had bought in the past. It came to the point that she could no longer support her mother's family so she had to concentrate on her own and that's when conflict with her own family started. They called her selfish and they would mock her, so she felt alone. Her husband Juan was off working in the mines of Winston, New Mexico and when he came back she took the biggest step of her life. During these years she had her second child her name was Maria and then they had their third Juan. Teresa decided that she would no longer be alongside her family. She felt used because all those years of supporting her family through thick and thin and when a bad time came they all blamed her for the downfall of the family. She decided that they would cross the border with the help of some of her friends.

Months of preparation were taken for the journey into the unknown. So one sunny hot day in Juarez, Teresa's mind was made up. She took her nineteen seventy six Ford Granada and she decided to cross. She had obtained permits for all of us to travel for six months, but we never came back after six months. Teresa ended up in a state called Washington in a little city called Yakima. She ended up in Yakima because her second to youngest sister had already made the journey. So she ended up in this town and things were really bad the first year. Juan, her husband, was unable to find work because of the lack of documentation. So the first couple of months were spent looking for places to stay and places where we could eat and find something to wear. Finally Teresa and Juan found a hotel on the outskirts of Yakima. It was a little miserable hotel, but to them it was home. Juan was making eighty dollars a week in one job, and a couple more in another job. He was working just to pay the days that they lived at the motel, but the kids were hungry and they needed other necessities like clothes and diapers, etc. So then a man that was really nice told Juan that he had job openings at a friend's of his orchard, picking and thinning and all kinds of stuff. So Juan accepted the offer and that was that. Juan was able to put food on the table and supply his family with the bare necessities.

The only problem was that they didn't have any papers to help them work legally in the United States. So then they heard over the radio that there was a period of time called the amnesty and then they decided to apply for legal documentation. Along with the help of a man named Salvador Herrera they were able to get their papers. So now they could work legally and the situation bettered for them and things were looking on the upside for once in a long time. What happened was really hard for them, but the living conditions were really poor.

There was no heating in this house so that winter was really harsh. They put plastic all around the windows to keep the heat in and they supplied themselves with a lot of blankets and stuff to keep themselves warm that winter. They got their kids in school so then they moved to another house. About two years after moving into that house, they moved to a house on Sixth Avenue in nineteen eighty six, and in nineteen eighty nine they purchased their very own house. It was then that the last of the children was born. His name was Alberto. She was filled with pride because this was the first of her children she didn't have to hide because she was not married to Juan. Things went pretty smooth. The pinnacle of her life was to see her oldest boy graduate. He graduated in nineteen ninety two from Davis High School in Yakima and then followed Maria in ninety five. Teresa has followed a very bumpy road all through her life, but now she owns two houses and has a child that will graduate in ninety nine and one more child who still has a long way to go. But she has the satisfaction that her children will have what she couldn't have, an education. I feel sorry to write this, but my mother's withered soul and body really don't have any other dreams but to rest because she has gone through a life of struggle and this struggle is nearing its end.

Celsa, Mi Madre

Omar Ramírez

Colima, a beautiful state, is located on the southern coast of México. The smallest state, but in value it is immense. Six kilometers north from the capital, (Colima) is a pueblo called Comala (borough of Comala), known as El Pueblo Blanco de América. On October 22nd, 1957, a girl named Celsa was born to Miguel Cruz Dueñas and to Modesta Montes Fuentes, the fifth daughter of the Cruz Montes family. There were thirteen children in all, seven barones and six hembras. Sardonically, two died over the time, one was Octavio who died in 1979, in a tragic car accident. And Alicia, the oldest in the family, died in October 5th, 1991, a drunk man took her life away with seven bullets.

At the age of four, Celsa was a bad child, she used to fight with Bertha, (her sister) over marbles. Modesta would hit her until she would listen. Celsa wouldn't listen to her mother because Miguel always did what Celsa said. Era una niña chiqueada con su papá. She was a mischievous girl who made capers to everyone en el barrio. Six years later she fought with kids in school because those kids would tease Bucho, a younger brother. The family was first in her life, she didn't care if the principal Mendoza would kick her out. Besides Celsa hated him; porque era muy malo y enojón con los niños, especialmente con ella.

One day it was her friend Martha's birthday party and the whole class got invited. Mario who liked Celsa was there also, and Sandra told Celsa about him. Her anger increased because Mario was the ugliest kid in the school. Concha and Celsa made a plan to make fun of Mario. Concha sets glue on Mario's chair, while Celsa called him to sit down. He gently sat down and Sandra was laughing, Mario didn't have a clue on what the heck everyone was laughing about. He couldn't stand up, he was stuck. Concha had poured lots of glue on the chair. Finally they had to cut his pants off, he was embarrassed. He had cried and cried because everyone in school knew about it, including Mr. Mendoza.

When she was sixteen, Celsa considered herself as a "cabroncita." She had dropped out of school to help the family. Every night she would go to the jardín with her friends. They pulled capers on the guys and had a good time. Braulio had three years of age, so Celsa sometimes took her brother to the jardín. Her dreams were to become a lawyer and to know el norte because she heard that el norte was the best place in the whole wide world. Sometimes she dreamed about a beautiful house on the hills where the view of Colima is seen. The illusions would never come true she thought. Since she dropped from school, she sold watermelons to people. "Era divertido trabajar," Celsa answered my question.

At age twenty, in 1977, she met Manuel Ramírez, a young man from Cualcomán, Michoacán. He had lived in Cowiche, Washington, for the last ten years, since his brother Juan's death. Celsa continued on her watermelon sales. Every single day Manuel would pass where she worked, con el pretexto de verla. He finally met Carmen, su apodo "La Mula." He sent letters to Celsa, la Mula was the bridge. Over the time Celsa fell in Love with Manuel, after he sent roses every day to her, even though he left to the U.S. each year. Felipa, "La Mosca," had major problems with Celsa sobre Manuel. In Comala, people used apodos (nicknames) instead of the real names. "Yo me enamoré de sus pantálones verdes de campana," she laughed. A macho from Michoacán. Dos años después sucede la tragedía de la famila, Octavio se murío en un maldito accidente, la fecha de la boda de Celsa y Manuel ya estaba fijada. El dieciseis de dicimbre de 1979, se cumplió un sueño grande para los dos, pero una melancolía por la muerte de Octavio.

Octavio era un gran hombre, él formó parte en la gran famila. Irónicamente el destino les jugó chueco. The celebration was awful, no music was heard from the wind of the surface. A road had formed an immense thorn in the hearts of el pueblo. "No era lo mismo sin Octavio, la alegría de la familia," she cried. A week later a honeymoon was planted on the laborious roads of the earth. Acapulco was the destiny of two humble lives. Followed by the voyage to Mexico City, where the cathedral, La Guadalupana, is located. Inolvidables momentos pasaron en el transcurso del pasaje sensacional. The dreams of oceans transformed into reality, after a dire life.

Omar, the first child of Manuel and Celsa was born on October sixth. He was born with celebral palsy, una enfermedad que cambió las vidas de la familia. Omar was supposed to be born a day before, but God wanted him this way. Celsa glanced to Memorial Hospital in Yakima, everyday to see her baby in tears. Three weeks without her boy, it felt like eternity. "Omar estaba entre la vida y la muerte, pero gracias a Dios todo salió bien," lloró la pobre madre. Six years passed. Celsa and Omar moved to Los Angeles, California, where Aldo was born. Manuel separated from Celsa. She was alone in the world, a profound anguish. Anulfo "La Mirla," Celsa's cousin, le extendió la mano. After the news of Aldo, Manuel begged perdón to her in tears. Life was amazing in California, but her life was in Yakima with the family. Omar and Aldo grew up with a tumor because they saw when Manuel hit Celsa. Omar wanted to die at the age of eight. No soportaba ver a sus padres peleándo como perro y gato.

She was thirty-one when Jessica arrived in their lives as a gift of heaven. December twenty-first, Jessica was born in Los Angeles, after another disengagement between Manuel and her. Besides Celsa had family in California, otherwise she would be trapped in a river. México, was the life for Omar, there he was isolated from the problems of the family. A temptation was set again in Celsa, to return to Los Angeles, where she had planted seeds of hope. Back again to Yakima, in 1989, Manuel had made a vow to her that they will always be together. But it didn't happen. No solution was based on the truth, only a journey back to Comala, set the illusion free. Turning points in their lives was made upon a world of hatred. Distinguish between callejones y caminos raros, una rosa dejó de florecer hace mucho tiempo. Celsa changed the world by returning to Yakima, in 1990.

Sor Juana was the image of Celsa. She had suffered in a fearful world in her mind. Malinche was compared to her, but she was not a backstabber to the fatherland. Different images took place in her life, "una vida amarga," she recalled with tristeza. For her sons, she was superior than all the great people in the universe, her hands are the food for her children and her tears are the water of the three kids of her heart.

The stage of forty years of life in the never ending world. Her palms are tired of working, it is not the same as before. Her back is hurting, el compromiso de la casa. The infancy had vanished from her life, "La vida es corta," a woman of honor wept. Los cruceros de calles se acábaron, nada es como antes, una niña muy feliz, un pueblo de bellos sueños. She had completed her dreams, her hijos are in school getting prepared for the real world. The only desire is to leave the great U.S. and move back to el pueblo. In spite of everything the woman had never regretted the life. Of course nothing would be the same in el pueblo, the osbtacles had taken her far away. "Es una vida pasajera, inolvidable vida," dijo la señora de mis sueños.

Enrique Castañeda Torres

Salvador Castañeda Muñiz

Born on November 5, 1951 in Santa Maria de Los Angeles, Jalisco, México. Enrique studied until his fourth year in school and then attended two years of high school where his favorite subjects were chemistry and mathematics. When Enrique was young he distributed ice cream to various stores. Some of his other jobs included gardening and then working for two years in a plastic manufacturing company when he was 18 years old.

In 1963, he went to the city of Guadalajara to look for better opportunities and development. During the 70's, he started to get involved in welding, pipe fitting, and designing print layouts. He worked as a welder making all kinds of machinery for different companies. He also says that he was making about five times the minimum wage. Enrique then started working on his own, making jobs for companies with other friends. He knew of this business through his friends.

In the early 1980's, his father, who was born in Texas, offered him a visa so Enrique could know what the U.S. was all about. Enrique was usually busy on his jobs and never imagined going to the U.S. He got the visas for all of us and we all came to California. He never thought that his father would be able to get the visas as fast as he did.

His job in California was with a company that made all kinds of sofas. There he made new machines to process the wood and gave them maintenance. He worked at that job for seven years. His biggest problem was not knowing English and he took some classes during night school, but he never really learned to communicate and keep a fluent conversation with English speaking people. He then got a job in a company named, "South Gate Engineering" and welded many kinds of projects, but that job only lasted for two years.

After many years of going back and forth between Guadalajara and the U.S., he ended up in Yakima, Washington. He never thought he would be working in one of the toughest jobs available, working in the orchards. That was the only job available to him. He had applied for a job in welding companies, but thinks he didn't get hired on because of his bad English.

"Working in the orchards isn't really that bad," is what he told me. "It's okay because you see all the people talking to each other, and then you get to breathe clean air." He says that his former job as a welder can be sometimes tougher than the orchards because it's dangerous to be around big machines. He says he still likes his former job and isn't willing to change his attitude about it. He says he has no other choice than to work on the orchards or in some canneries until he learns to speak English. He says he is making sacrifices for us, because he knows that school in the United States is good and we (his kids) need to do whatever is possible to succeed and take all of the opportunities that stand in our way and not let them go.

Meanwhile, Enrique likes to keep up to date with what is going on in the world. He reads the Yakima Herald every morning. He can read in English and understand most of it, but isn't able to speak it at a normal pace. He likes spending time exploring the internet and reading about new technology that is coming out.

I sometimes underestimate my father because I think he doesn't know how to do some of my homework. I'm taking some advanced classes but the old man knows how to do it. I get surprised by all of the things he knows. For not attending college, that's awesome. He knows much about math and chemistry and sometimes I challenge him with a question and then he challenges me with another of his own. It's always a battle, but the old man always seems to win me.

His favorite music group are called, "Los Babies." His favorite foods are "caldo de res," cooked fish and Cornish hens. His favorite color is green. He doesn't drink or smoke. And his last remark for the class is to keep on studying because it can be very tough without it. He tells everyone to take all the opportunities that this country has. There are many opportunities and it is very rich and if you take your chances and keep going forward, you can make your life much easier in the near future.

The Interview

Natalia Castañeda

I interviewed my uncle who is a farmworker. Su nombre completo es Antonio Figueroa Cortez, su fecha de nacimiento es Junio 13 de 1951.

This is what he said...

"The farmwork is hard, I worked in farm work for 14 years. The farmworker is not different than the work from el Rancho. It's the same thing. You pick up what you grow. The only difference is that you work here for other people and you get money for what you do, and in México you work for your own food. You don't have a patrón in México."

He said, "If I had the choice I would have preferred to have my own business, any kind of business. When I work in the apples, I don't pick anymore. I operate the tractor and mow the lawn, but when I operate the tractor, my job is to carry the big boxes of apples and take them. Every summer that's what I do, I drive the tractor."

"It all happened because the man that used to drive it left the job and since the boss knew me for almost 10 years, and was a real good friend of mine, he changed me. The pay was better because when I picked apples they paid me six dollars an hour, and now they pay me ten. I wouldn't go back to picking apples even if they paid me ten dollars. One of my dreams is to go back to México and have my own ranch with cows, horses, hens, pigs, goats, and all kinds of animals. I wouldn't encourage anybody to be a farmworker."

"It's a hard job and it affects the organism. I would encourage people to study and get a good education and a good job without going to the fields. I have had some good experiences also. I have learned a lot from this. I never thought I would be here with all of these apples and different kinds of fruits.

"La pisca es sin duda un trabajo muy pesado y sin embargo como lo dice ésta entrevista lo dice, hay mucha gente que lo hace para seguir adelante.

Interview with Natalio Roque

Teresa Roque

July 27, 1956, Natalio Días was born. He's the fourth of 12 children, but only eight survived. At the age of eight years old he started to work in his home town doing odd jobs.

Living with his grandparents, he took care of a fleet of lambs they owned. At the age of 15 he decided to try his luck in another country, a country he knew very little about—just that it was the country of gold.

"Water was reaching to our shoulders. I tried to cross the river that would get me into the United States," Natalio told me. Natalio was nervous because he never imagined crossing a hot desert, crossing some parts of the desert where rain storms happened. Night came and he and the others that came with the group had to rest. They circled the campground with rocks and on top they added a small amount of garlic on top so no snakes would come near them.

His first job was picking lemons and doing other odd jobs.

"It was an OK job, but the first days were horrible. My hands were all scratched up by the branches. I made some money to get along with. Waking up at 5:00 and returning to our cabins after 6:00 or later at night, it depended on what the rancher wanted us to do. I hated the way I thought, because I came to look for a better life and all I found was working harder than ever."

Natalio stayed in Arizona for some months, and then he was invited by some friends to come farther up North to Idaho.

At first his job was turning on and off the irrigation water for the crops. After a short time in the harvesting of potatoes, he worked in the warehouse just checking how the potatoes weighed. "The work was not that hard, but the pay, they paid us every two weeks. When we had any food left, some of my friends would cook potatoes, and we would just eat them like that, and that was our dinner."

Natalio got tired of the work he was doing. He heard some of his friends say that in the State of Washington is where the apples were, and that there the money came in easy. And so again he decided to try his luck in Yakima. Arriving in Yakima, they rented an apartment with his friends. They started looking for a job, until they came to Naches. There he worked picking apples. "I got up at 5:30 to get to the ranch at 6:00. There I worked under the hot sun. At lunch time I ate with my hands dirty, since there was no water to wash off. At the end of the day I would have around 13 bins done. I was fast at picking apples."

Since Natalio came to this country he hardly had a moment that someone was racist against him. "A horrible time that I lived through was the explosion of Mt. St. Helens." I thought it was the end of the world. I was scared. I went to the airport to get a ticket. I wanted to get out of Yakima, but the lady said that the airport was closed. I returned home. I prayed that day until I fell asleep. I never would like to go through that day again."

What would you tell a young man that would like to come to the United States? I asked him.

"I would tell him that coming to the United States is not easy. It's not what people say it is. And if you come, never forget where you came from. Many people come to the United States to work to have money to support their families, but others just come to give us Mexicans a bad name. But the one things is, never forget your cultures. And never forget the hard work it takes to come and reach the American Dream."

Jesús Gil Navarro

Jesús Gil

My father's name is Jesús Gil Navarro. He was born in a ranch called, "La Cuestita." He is 38 years old, and he thinks that he is old already. My father told me that when he was a boy, he and his brothers always were working in the cerro, con el azadón sembrando el maíz. My father said, "Que la vida de antes era más difícil, que la de hoy. This is because they didn't have school to go to and because they always were in the cerro working. My dad decided to come to the United States because he was tired of working every day in the same cerro. Él se desesperaba por que a veces no tenía dinero ni para los "chicles." The first time that he came to the United States he was 16 years old, and he came by himself without papers.

El estaba seguro, de que él podía llegar a su destino con la bendición de su madre. He said that it was easy to cross the frontera, because he was looking how other people were crossing it. Él dijo que se juntó con otras personas, que también querían cruzarse y que de volada se pasaron sin tener problemas. I asked to my father, "You never got lost on the way to the Norte?" and he said, "No, por que preguntando se llega a Roma."

The time passed by and he made his dream become true in coming to the United States. Cuando empezó a trabajar juntando nueces él se sentía felíz, emocionado, por que andaba trabajando en el famoso Norte. Pero su sueño de él no terminaba juntando nueces el quería a venir Washington a cortar manzanas. El venía con muchas ganas de trabajar por que él quería ayudar a sus papas a salir adelante.

His parents were very poor, sometimes they ate tacos de sal. He didn't like to see his little brothers with ripped clothing, that's why he decided to come to the Norte. He said that if his parents would have had a better way of life, he wouldn't come to the United States.

When he started working in the campo él miró que los patrones de aquí nomás andaban atrás de las personas, mirando el trabajo que ellos andaban haciendo. Los patrones son más exigentes, quieren el trabajo muy bien hecho. En México los patrones eran más buenas gentes, después del trabajo que hacíamos, cortando el maíz, ellos nos llevaban sodas, dulces, para el que quisiera. In México we weren't thinking about the patrón. We weren't intimidated by his presence."

Cuando mi papá estaba aprendiendo más acerca del norte, él miraba que les pagaban muy barato y que los ponían a trabajar por mucho tiempo. Él no decía nada, él nada más trabajaba más duro, para mandarle dinero a sus papás. Al poco tiempo él se empezó a dar cuenta de que extrañaba a sus padres, él ya se quería regresar para su tierra, pero no podía, por que tenía que trabajar. Los primeros dos años que él estuvo por acá se le hicieron eternidades. When he went back to México, he only stayed for a while and he didn't like living here anymore. The time passed by and my dad brought us to this country to live with him.

From My Uncle to the World

Raúl Chacón

This interview took place between two places: Freeway 12 at West Yakima and the Chesterly Park at 40th Avenue. When I started asking my questions, my uncle was driving his troca. My purpose on this interview is to know his point of view about fields.
How old are you, Uncle?
Why do you want to know? ¡Cabrón!
Because I'm going to do a homework.
¡Homework! About what?
About someone who works at the fields.
But what do you want to know?
Everything. Like why you came to the U.S.A., working conditions, Comparisons between el Rancho in México, and the life here, in a few words, all about your life.
I understand you now, "Guey."

"Look! Me, Andres Chacon-Vargas. I was born in a small Ranch called "Ticuelaca," very close to Coalcoman Michoacán, México in May 1952. During the first 20 years of my life I worked in "Ticueluca" with many different "caciques" but "La pinche miseria que pagaban no me alcanzaba para pagar."

"In 1972 I decided to come here, because a lot of people told me about this place, like jobs, good salary, and good life but, they never told me about "La pinche migra." They caught me, it was in 1975. I was working in Naches, WA. Here comes "la migra" one of the workers said. Me and your brother José run toward a long "canal de agua." I jumped in it but your brother didn't. In the apple fields everybody was running in all directions through other fields. That day no one had escaped, just me and your brother. I was so stupid, because later in the day I went to Yakima, WA. I had to put some gasoline in my car, I was at a 7-11 seven-eleven by Yakima Avenue. There the "migra" caught me. They took me to Wapato's jail. I spent one night in Wapato's jail, then they took me to Seattle, and then to Mexicali's border. During the journey from Wapato to Mexicali, they just gave me an orange juice and an apple.

"I arrived to Mexicali como a las 3 de la mañana. But in the same day I rode the bus to Tijuana. In Tijuana there were many persons trying to cross the border. In July, 1972 I crossed the border with many other persons. I had to pay $250 dollars. The "Coyote" took us to L.A. He was "a toda Madre" because he gave me no food during three days. In L.A. I stayed just three days and in the fourth day one of my friends named Daniel gave me a ride to Yakima, WA. When I arrived in Yakima, WA I looked for a job but I didn't find one until one week later. During that week my house was a cherry tree and my bathroom was the Naches River. But in 1988 mi vida changed. I started working with "Allan Brothers" in Naches, WA. I worked very hard, and the same time I was learning how to speak English. I never went to school. I learned English by listening to my bosses. It wasn't easy. I felt like a stranger because I didn't understand "ni Madres." I think that the job is better and different here than México because there in México, you kill yourself working and trying to make a fuckin Peso. At least here you work, and have hopes that one day the Social Security will be giving money to you. The year of 1988 changed my life because I became resident of this country, and the same year "The Allan Brothers" gave me the job of foreman on one of their ranches in Naches, WA.

Later in 1996 I went to study citizenship class at Davis High School. After my job I went to school at night for about one month. In the same year I became a citizen of this country, and I'm still working for Allan Brothers Company. So what? "Guey," es todo lo que me acuerdo.

OK "Tillito." Thanks a lot.

An Interview with Mother

Eva Siddhartha Valdivia

Where were you born?
    Tinajas, Colima, México

When?
    September 13, 1939

Were you born in a hospital or at home?
    At home.

How was it where you were born, did you like it?
    Era un rancho. Rodeado de animales que criábamos para comer nosotros y vegetales que crecíamos. En aquel tiempo no teníamos lo que ustedes tienen ahora. No tele, no radio, no teléfono. Teníamos, bueno más bien hicimos un pozo de agua para tener para nosotros y canales para regar las plantas y vegetales. Era muy duro aquel tiempo. Yo me compadezco de mi madre, por tenernos a todos y poder hacer tanto por sus

hijos, como quisiera que todavía estuviese viva.

¿Fuiste a la escuela?
Al principio no. Pero después a mi madre se las ingenió para que nosotros los más chicos tan siquiera, pudieramos asistir aunque fuera a escondidas de tu abuelo. *Tu abuelo no tenía abuela.* Sólo quería que nos quedáramos en casa todo el tiempo como esclavas. En realidad eso éramos tu madre y yo... Hice mi escuela en Colima hasta el quinto grado. Después nos fuimos a Morelia donde asistí a la Universidad de Michoacán pero me faltaron dos años para acabar.

¿Por qué no acabaste?
Porque tuve a tu hermana y despuesito a ti. Estuve muy ocupada y me afligí mucho. Necesitaba dinero y tenía que encontrar una manera de hacerlo para darles lo que necesitaban. Nunca me había sentido tan mal pues a mi no me gusta estorbar a nadie y causar molestias. Tu madre me estaba ayudando en ese tiempo tan duro, pero no quería ser un estorbo..

¿Qué no te casaste?
No, ninguna de las dos veces.

¿Por qué, que pasó?
Pues, eso es una gran historia que no tiene caso recordar. Pero si te digo, que lo único es que querían que nos casaramos por la iglesia lo cual yo a ese tiempo me estaba aislando.

Entonces, me podrías decir ¿Quién es mi papá?
Bueno y que lo vas ir a buscar. Pues en realidad, no se por qué te preocupa saber, de alguien que no se intereso por ti. Pero bueno, si quieres apuntar, el se llama o se llamaba Victor Manuel Olivar.

¿De donde es?
Lo conocí en Guadalajara. El trabajaba en Salubridad en el hospital general en aquel tiempo. Ha de tener entre 52-58 años de edad. No sé si viva o tenga familia. Ese es el único lugar donde sabía encontrarlo.

¿El sabía, o sabe que yo existo?
No.
¿Por qué no?
No se lo dijé porque no se lo merecía.

¿Entonces, como esperabas que él se procupara o se interesara, en mí, si ni siquiera sabía él de mi existencia?
Pues no sé. El sabía era médico. Tal vez se hizo el tonto.

Por favor me diras en realidad lo que pasó.
Para qué, no vale la pena.

¿En qué trabajas?
Era Secretaria de Gobierno el el estado de Michoacán. Pero cuando fui a Guadalajara trabajé en el hospital general, donde conocí desafortunadamente a tu padre.

¿Te gustaba tu trabajo?
Pues sí, pero todo era tan corrupto que decidí dejar eso. Además no era suficiente el pago.

¿Eras muy política verdad?
Pues a mí sólo me gustaba aclarar las cosas. Me da mucho coraje cuando la gente no cumple con su palabra. Me gustaba desenmascarar a la gente mentirosa que tenía poder sobre la gente humilde, pero ya ahora eso se lo dejo a Jehova Dios.

¿Platícame,¿Cómo era mi abuelo?
Un patán. Le hacía la vida imposible a mi mamá. Era celoso. Por culpa de él ella falleció. Sabes, ni me menciones de él porque si estuviera aquí, le diría muchas cosas. Ya que se iba a morir yo le perdoné, pero con muy pocas ganas.

¿Cómo era mi abuela?
Una maravilla. La quise mucho y como desearía deseo que estuviese aquí conmigo. Era una mujer muy trabajadora. Siempre se las ingeniaaba para que nosotros tuviéramos hasta más de lo necesario. Pero era muy difícil para ella.
Especialmente por tu abuelo que le hacía la vida imposible. Mi madre era una gran mujer de admirar. Trabajaba tan duro cada

día, y nunca paraba. Primero Dios, la tenga en su gloria

Sé que hubo una etapa en la cual te desesperaste por el dinero, y decidiste venir a los Estados Unidos. ¿Por qué me dejaste?

¡Hay hijita! Eso es algo que jamás me voy a perdonar ni a mí misma. Estabas muy chiquita y pensé que era mejor. No quería que nada te pasara al cruzar andando con gente desconocida. Además yo pensaba regresar por ti lo antes posible, pero no fue así..Había muchas cosas envueltas. No tenía el dinero. No tenía el dinero necesario. Apenas tenía lo suficiente para comer tu hermana y yo. En eso me arrepiento mucho. Pues, no te educaron como yo lo quería y te alejaron del Dios, que yo ahora conozco, Jehova.

¿Por qué no luchas por tus sueños?

Hago lo posible, pero yo vivo en la harmonia de Dios. Él hará de mí lo que él quiera, yo haré lo que él desee. Viéndolo bien yo si persigo mis sueños. Mi sueño es estar con Dios, más bien al lado de Dios cuando éste mundo se acabe que será muy pronto, y quiero ganarme mi lugar ahí. Lo demás es lo de menos.

Disculpa el carácter de está pregunta. ¿Pero en otras palabras te importa un comino lo que le pase a mi hermano y a mi?

Por supuesto que me importa. Pero si Dios me pidiera que le diera en sacrificio yo lo haría. Así como Abraham lo hizo con su hijo.

¿Si tú pudieras empezar de nuevo que cambiarías?

Todo, menos mi creencia en Dios y el ser Testigo de Jehová.

¿Por qué no tuviste más hijos como la mayoría a costumbra tener?

Primeramente el tener a ustedes dos y sin lazos matrimoniales es algo que pagué y sigo pagando muy alto. Tener hijos y sin los dos padres presentes es muy difícil. A mí, no me hubiera gustado tener de un montón, porque sé lo difícil que es vivir modestamente. Yo quiero lo mejor para ustedes. A veces la gente que tiene muchos hijos me da mucho coraje. Pues ya no estamos en los tiempos de antes donde la religión misma, "católica" prohibía el cuidado para no tener hijos. A mi sólo me da tristeza, porque veo a muchos jóvenes tan perdidos, haciendo quien sabe Dios de barabaridades, y los padres no los reprimen, sólo se quejan.

¿Sabes mamá, admiro tu devoción inmensa hacia Dios, pero no te parece que es demasiado aquí en la tierra con los humanos?

Lo sé, pero sólo hay alguien que me comprende y que sabe por qué hago las cosas que hago. Y en realidad con eso a mí me basta. Con que él sepa me conformo, porque esa es mi fé y mi fé mueve montañas.

¿Te llevabas bien con mis Tíos, tus hermanos?

Si, todos nos ayudamos siempre. Eramos muy apegados. Después de que nuestra madre murió todos nos fuimos por distintos caminos y todo cambió. Tu madre era la única ayuda que yo tenía. Aunque a veces nos comunicamos, tus tíos se hicieron mas distantes desde la primera vez que yo rehusé lazos matrimoniales.

¿Que le pasó a mi Tío Maximiliano?

Él un día se quiso venir para acá, y se vino en barco, pero nunca supimos más de él. Dos o tres meses después de que se vino nos avisaron que el barco se había hundido y todos abordo fallecieron. Tu abuela casi se volvió loca todos lo queríamos mucho. Él era el más pequeño y el más guapo. Él y yo casi estábamos más juntos pues éramos los más chicos. Yo resentí mucho su perdida. A veces quiero pensar que está vivo y por un rato lo hago, pero sé que no es real.

¿Te gustaría regresar a México?

Cuando me muera quisiera ser enterrada allá, pero ahorita como está la situación, no. Aquí hay más oportunidades, por eso quise que ustedes estuvieran aquí para aprovechar. La economía está por los suelos allá. En realidad sea donde sea me da igual.

¿Por qué no te has casado?

Porque no he encontrado a la persona correcta.

¿Pero, cómo la vas a encontrar si no te haces disponible?

En realidad no me interesa. No estoy en busca y no lo estaré.

¿No te sientes sola?

No, yo tengo a Jehová Dios a mi lado. ¿Qué más quiero? Yo soy feliz con tal de saber que ustedes estén bien y cerca de mi. Sólo me entristece que ustedes no estén sirviendo en Betel, como yo hubiera querido con los Testigos de Jehova. Pero bueno, todavía no es el fin. Primero Jehová Dios.

III. Poems

How can one's childhood
be a dangerous enemy?

Alma Varela

Looking for America

Salvador Sanchez

I hear me winning a race in running.
I see the world and I understand it.
I remember the mistakes I made
and try to fix them.
I think I can go to college
and be successful.
I feel surprised that I have gone
this far in life.
I want to explore everything
and learn everything.
I love running and innovating.
I want to be the best that I can be.
When I fall down I get right back up.
I can hear my family
be proud, and I am proud.

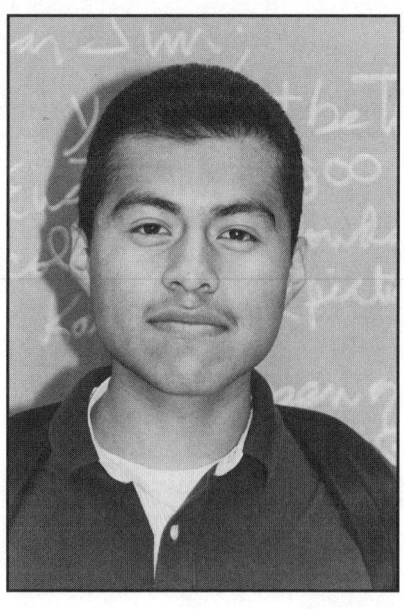

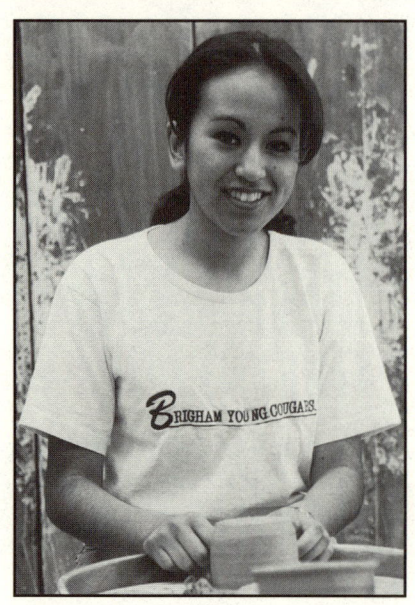

A Suite of Five Poems

Alma Varela

53rd Birthday

She kills a rooster and makes mole,
For her birthday dinner
Maria's hoping for me to call her.

Her daughters are all away,
Her daughters are all blind
Her daughters are far in the U.S.
Her daughters are…

They will be back
When there's no other better choice.

Las hijas son ingrates
Las hijas de María.

She killed a rooster today
To eat a table of seven
And only three chairs are pulled out.

She killed a rooster today
Saying look INS, look!
As she cuts across its throat.
Warm fumes appear within the air.

She knows how,
My mother knows how to kill a rooster
Or a gallina or a conejo.

She killed a rooster just as I was stopped
at the light of /Tieton and 16th.

TRANSPORTATION

A regular day at San Lázaro
You watch cars go by 60-70 miles per hour
Where pedestrians are supposed to have the right of way
And are forced to wait
Breathing the gray air transmitting vomiting smells
Of everyone else's lives, running fast on the streets.

Right behind San Lázaro;
The place where people come and go,
Far and close, is the airport.

Airplanes take off, very elegantly looking
To a far distant place.
The subway runs under the city,
Not a pin can fit in it after its first stop.

The micros are the small versions of a clean bus.
500 pesos and you sometimes get to sit down.

The Ruta 100 is for everybody. 100 pesos and you're home,

All you do is wait in the line for about 45 minutes.

A guy selling peanuts goes by,
The guy selling frozen suckers goes by
The kids who polish shoes go by and
The man with no legs brings his guitar
And a metal can.

Behind, in Candelaria Avenue
Is another whole gathering of people,
Over 18 usually.
It's lots of women with very short skirts,
Big boobs and tiny bras.

A bunch of hombres gather around,
Watching their spectacular nature.
The 65-year-old man takes one of them
By the hand, the youngest one and
Around the street they go looking for a motel,
All between fruit stands

San Lazaro is called
"The place where people,
Children, women and men go,
Looking for
Transportation,

One sells sex
One sells peanuts
One sells frozen suckers
One sells childhood
One sells his voice
One takes an airplane a long distance
One takes a micro to pass by as if he's middle class.
One takes the subway going around in circles while
Someone else might jump under it for an even
Faster transportation.
Another one takes a Ruta 100 because he's
Stuck with only 100 pesos.
Maybe he wants to eat roasted peanuts on the way home.

Maybe he wants to hear the man without legs
And his guitar sing as he slides
Through, laying on a wooden board with
Little wheels under it.

There is transportation even standing there,
Looking.

OPPOSITES

Why are they crossing the border?
Why are they illegal?
Why don't they speak English?
      They are so dark.
Let's fire them.
Let's throw them out.
Let's build a higher fence.
Let's make another law.
Let's make them work like fucking burros.
But why are they taking our jobs?

Why don't you cross the border?
Why aren't you illegal?
Why don't you speak Spanish?

You are beautiful.
Let's not throw you out.
Let's hire you.
Let's tear down the fence.
Let's make one world of diversity.
Let's work together.

Many places have seen such criticism
Many places have changed their way of living
Their way of thinking, their way of being
Walls have come down
The Berlin Wall came down in Germany

No more Cold War,
No more Iron Curtain,

One people, living, surviving,
Clinging to hope…for
Posterity and happiness.

For this, we all should know that
We are the beautiful Mexicanos.
        Why not?

LIKE THIS

There are nights   like this
That I am   a cat,
Sitting   on the rusty moon

Holes   in them let the air
Go through   and
I breathe.

Sitting   on a rusty moon
Looking   for the next sky.

A halo that encircles   dancing words
In my head   telling the news.

There are nights   like this
That I am   a cat
Sitting   on a rusty moon.

SOCCER GAME

I was on the other side of the fence
Of the soccer field.

The air felt a part of me and touched
The body under my blue hat.

Walking towards the entrance
I looked down and saw my white socks
Through the hole in my right tennis shoe.

As I looked up, my left hand reached
The blue back pocket of my jeans.

Then I took out three green pieces of paper.
"It's sort of like a *fun* raiser," the lady at the door said.

Towards the sky the lights were on, lighting the field,
Delivering the sense of a summer day

Down on the left end of the field
The goalie was shouting,

"Tírala hijo, eso es todo Momia."

The black and yellow letters glowing across his chest read

        MÉXICO

So I sat down and folded my hat curved
on my forehead.

From Gavicel's Poetry Notebook

Gavicel Antúñez

May 15, 1998

Everybody in this world has different mysteries. We must know that we need to share what we're thinking each day. Everybody has something to say. Mr. Grimes always with his smile when he is reading, always going to the past, something that he will not forget, getting news from his poems. It's a mystery for us because it's not always the same thing, life changes, and it will keep going. We can't stop the good times, not even the bad times, always something happens in our lives. If we shared with others, it helps, like medicine, always making people comfortable, always doing something each day, and each day we learn something. Today is my last day to give my work to Mrs. Bernazzani. I have to do my homework after school. Today I send in my scholarship, this is the first one, but I didn't do well, but who cares, I just send it.

May 16, 1998

Today, a special day, my cousin came, and my friend came. It was fun because they eat, then we went to play basketball. Together we talk about the Bible, and about my graduation. They are so happy because they know that I will graduate two weeks later, they know that. What I know now is that they have a surprise for me for that day. I'm kind of exited because I will receive my diploma. But I don't want to go that fast I want to stay for ever where I'm at now, here at Davis High School. But who knows what is going to happen? Nobody, nobody in this world knows that, I have tears in my eyes but what can I say and do, the only thing is wait and see what is coming next. I will miss my teachers all my teachers, every single one I will have in my mind. I will think, I will see a different world around me, different people, different faces, friends I will lose. How is it going to be, when the time passes? Good question to myself.

May 17, 1998

Today Sunday. A nice day with dark clouds, I wake up at 9 something. The thing was that I had a bad dream probably because I didn't pray, that's what my mom told me. It was scary, I went to church first at 4:30 with sister Silvia but she was not there so me and my mother and brother went to play basketball but it was kind of cold so we didn't play, but I did my math work, just a little not that much. Then at 7:00 we went to church, then I helped them collect the money. Then I passed the people to communion, so I did. We went home and my mom ate with my brother, but I didn't eat. Everybody was mad at me, even my dad, but so what, I explained to them that I had homework to do but they didn't understand that. Sometimes they see that I don't eat and they are worried about me. I like when they worry about me. I'm saying this with a big smile. They understand me.

May 25, 1998

Today was a nice day. Everybody was happy, my mom, my dad, my brother. I was kind of sad because my dad took my brother to work, I don't like that because my dad does hard work. In my mind I always said, "Why he works in asparagus." It's too hard, my dad used to take me, now he wants to do the same, I know he will but I'm not scared, now I will only worry about graduating but then where will I go? What I will do next? Always listen to my dad without any hope for us. Always he worries about his payments. Today was very fun, I played tennis with my brother and two friends of his. Today I did my homework trying to figure out Math problems and trying to do my Accounting, but in the end I didn't do anything.

May 26, 1998

Thinking now, one problem I have in my life is between my mom, and dad. I'm always asking help for myself, not asking for someone else. The most important is that I love my mom and my dad. Now the time is passed and I have not done anything. Well I can do something, but yes I could do something but like what? I don't have ideas. My dad doesn't talk to my mom, why I don't know, well I don't have to think that because sometimes he does, he gets mad very fast. Why, I don't know, probably he is tired, who knows, now I'm painting a picture, I could forget my problems. When I draw or paint different colors, sometimes I give dad headaches but who cares—"my mom I know". Today I will stay after school. What happened today? I have tears in my eyes but nobody sees it, each tear that I drop I make it in a big smile with others. I don't even understand myself. Why this happens to me I don't understand. I mean be with hard heart, well probably not, because the only who sees me cry is my mom, but she knows why.

May 30, 1998

Today was sunny with some people walking through the roads with friends or some people just doing exercises, walking or jumping or driving bikes. Today I went to the mail box and I received my application from college. I sent them the form but they didn't receive it so I have it now but I will send it back in some couple of months. For right now, I first will work and then I will do something for me, that's life. Today I was waiting for my dad because he told us that he was going to take us, so we did about everything, we were close. Today I went to a quinceañera, it was fun because everything was silence in the Church, her dress was white with green flowers, it was pretty she was just a friend. My brother wanted to go to dance, but just because of my dad we didn't go.

"I Found Myself"

I found myself on the mall
I look at myself in a mirror
I was standing in the hall
I wanted to disappear
I wanted to hide myself
I couldn't look in the mirror
then I realized by myself
I was the only one
everybody wanted to be near.

"I found myself"

Mystery

Looking through my
plate is what I love
because I have my own
food. Yep my delicious
plate, my favorite
plate. Who knows how
to make it, my mom,
of course. What question!

Questions I don't have
a lot, most of my questions
I gave answered always In my life.

Belief is what I have
I believe and I have
hope in my life.

And I know you have
hope in your life too.

Gavicel Antúñez

My Grandma's Favorite Gorditas

Biatriz Díaz

On Saturday
a comfortable afternoon
after a hard week,
A cool resting time.
My Grandma has come
to visit us, even my
cat named Popis
feels her visit.
Our warm welcoming
for Grandma is a pleasant
ocean of cinnamon
warm blessings and words.

I had promised her
I would cook for her
Gorditas de harina,
during her presence.
Most beloved by her.
She had made herself
a home already. She
was sitting on a rocking
chair out on the porch,
receiving the air of our
love for her, and the
oxygen of our spirits
surrounding her.
All of a sudden
a very tempting aroma
of sugar mixed with
flour and oil starts
calling my Grandma's
attention.
I would always ask
her, "Would you like to
have one of my Gorditas

Grandma?" And I remember
my Grandma answering,
"My diet wouldn't, but
my mouth can't resist."

Just a Few Words
Un Poema, Un Consejo,
Una Palabra, Un Hecho
A Poem, An Advice
A Word, Something Done

Samuel Barrera

No es bueno—de un amor imposible. No es bueno dar la vida entera en algo que te destruye, que te aflige, que te agota. Es bueno encontrar el camino que te lleva al triunfo, quitar la piedra del camino para que otros no tropiecen, y dejar un machete afilado para un nuevo abrecaminos. No, no es bueno querer alcanzar el cielo without dreams of success. Never throw a rock in the air if that rock will harm you and others. No es bueno caminar descalzo sobre montones de botellas llenas de sueños. Prisioneros por el miedo de experimentar. There are flowers that with love they grow fresh and green again y en cambio hay corazones que están muriendo de amor.

In the whole world there are beauties, but none like a woman. El abrazo más bueno es el que te da la vida cada vez que sale el sol. El despertar del día es el comienzo de la jornada. I'd rather see your soul with the eyes of mine y es bueno cantar alegre con el corazón abierto. Life is an embrace of opportunities. Preparation is the first sentence on an infinite paragraph that should have a great, good conclusion.

Conclusion is what you overcome to finish your preparation.

La mejor arma y aún más poderosa es la comunicación es algo que tiene que ver con el éxito del mundo entero unido como uno solo, que es. When you are writing for a while and you feel that your mind is blank, it is not true. What happens is that there is a lack of communication between both. Un error en un trabajo no significa que lo pudiste hacer mejor, y por ese error lo es.

Sudor significa que estás haciendo un buen trabajo y tu cuerpo te lo agradece. Sweat means that you are doing good work, and your body thanks you. El orgullo más grande que tengo es ser yo mismo. Así ¿soy y qué? So what?

Quien lucha siempre, frente a frente y no se vence es un héroe para él mismo, para siempre. Who always fights face to face, and never gives up, is a hero for himself forever.

Sometimes I'm sorry might mean I will do it again, so be careful.

The most famous frase is "querer es poder" y si se quiere se puede. What you do best is what you do and care about. Abre tu ventana al conocimiento y a la verdad. Todavía estoy soñando con la mañana en mis brazos. A few words speak more than themselves. Pocas palabras hablan más que sí misma.

Un beso es el reflejo del cariño valiente en nuestros corazones. La mente es una—de ideas y verdades que hay que saber—. Mi error fue cometarlo y negarlo. Love is like a rose. It lives, it dies and it grows green and fresh again with more life. El error de la mentira es ocultar siempre verdad.

Una buena obra no construye casas sino puentes the amistad. El pasado es el mito del hombe. El hombre fue ayer, es hoy mañana y siempre. Hambre es querer satisfacerce de sueños y hacerlos realidad para triunfar en la vida.

Éxito significa empezar, expresar lo que sentimos/pensamos, tener una buena tención. Trabajar siempre duro sin negarse aún si hay fracasos, o retardos. Otorgarse un abrazo felicitandonos a nosotros mismos—que—alcanzado.

Triunfo significa lo hice aún con miedo, confíe en mi mismo, intenté una y otra vez hasta que todo salió 100.99% y lo logré.
What do you think?
Your opinion can make a big difference in someone's life.

Believe In Me

Jacqueline Hernández

I try to think and think
and I never come up with
a solution to our relations,
to our problems. I can't
understand why we treat each other
the way we do?
You should be the person
I should love the most.
You should be the person
I should trust with everything.
I should be the person
you should believe in.
But no, you prefer to
believe in others.
You prefer to think the worst of me,
you never believe in my word.
I always told you the truth,
and if now sometimes I lie to you,
it's because you made me.
The way you treat me,
the way you think of me,
you don't deserve other than that.

But I am not like you,
I like to play clean.
I know I have to respect you
even though you don't respect me,
even if I don't like the way you are,
I have to be with you.
You gave me what nobody could give me,
for that I have to thank you, and I do.
But don't treat me
the way you do.
Don't rule over me
the way you do.
Just because you are my mother.

Why Did You Leave Me?

Nobody has hurt me
as you had.
Nobody has done to me
what you had.
In my mind, there is always a voice
repeating your name.
And always the same questions.
Where are you?
Why did you leave?
Who did you prefer instead of me?
Why did you abandon me?
If you knew that you were
what I needed the most,
what I miss more than anything?
I'll never forget your abandonment.
You hit me very hard with it.
Yet, I always carry you with me.
You are something that even
if I wanted
I couldn't take out of me.
You are part of me.
I am your blood.
Thanks to you, I exist.
But I didn't ask you for my life
so that you could leave me

without giving me an explanation.
I forgive you for everything
you have done to me
and I will love you all my life
and beyond if there is
life after death, FATHER.

MY PEN IS MY VOICE

René Guzmán

All people have different ways to
use their voice. "I" has so many
writers. My pen is my voice.

Because in every poem, in every letter,
in every paragraph, and in every sentence,
I express my voice and people hear me.

I'm quiet, true, but my pen is my voice.
And nobody can take that from me.
Only when I die, but maybe, I'm not sure.

For teachers, teaching is their voice.
For artists, painting or drawing is their voice.
For writers, the pen is their voice.

I write more and I talk less
because my pen is my voice
and it would be forever.

POEMS BY CARLOS GONZALEZ

THE TRIP LOOKING FOR WHO I AM

"…entered each man like a short lance."
       Pablo Neruda

I was in Michoacán living with my grandparents.
Everything was really good when I was
a little kid, but, when I grew up,
the problems came to me.
I have an uncle, he is 5 years older than me.
We had to fight for everything,
no matter what simple things.
He was always mean to me,
telling me things for being in his
parent's house.
Everytime that he got mad, he
called me "Arrimado." It means be living
in a house that is not yours.
He also made me do "quehaceres,"
things that had to be done by him in the house,

for example, I had to feed the pigs and cows.
True, he taught me to drive.
I had to do things for him, in exchange.
He could hit me anytime that he wanted,
and I couldn't do nothing back
to him because he could correrme
of his house, something that made me feel so bad.
Sometimes it made me cry, because
I didn't want to come to United States.

Three Letter Poems to Three Latinas

Letter to Gloria Anzaldúa, Strong, Rebelde and Woman

¿Cómo te gusta la mala vida? This question
encierra many different meanings to me.
I am a young man, and during my 20 years
of life, I am seeing how difficult is the

life for a woman. Like in my ranchito,
where I come from, a small town in Michoacán,
men still think that women are only
for making tortillas, to take care of the babies,

and to be in the house. It seems like
you say, "Women have had three ways to go:
to the Church as a nun, to the streets
as a prostitute, or to the home as a

mother." In my ranchito, a woman can not
even think of study. "That is wrong," men
say, because she is going to lose her time.
Why study, if she is the one who will be

in the home all the time when she gets married?
The men always say to the women, "Tu no
sirves pa' nada" besides cooking and cleaning,

"Eres pura vieja."

No puedes vivir con ellas y sin ellas."
¿Entonces por qué el hombre trata con
tanta diferencia a la mujer, si la necesita?

"If a woman remains a virgin until she
marries, she is a good woman." I know this.
No estoy de acuerdo con ésto. OK, a woman
has to be a virgin when she gets married,

to be a good woman, but what about the
men? A man can have sex with more than
one woman before he gets married, but he
still is asking for a virgin woman.

Yo siendo un hombre, no puedo entender
esta parte de la vida, no puedo cambiar
ésto pero al menos trataré de vivir mejor
que esto. Gloria,

me haces muy feliz el saber que aún
hay mujeres como tú en el mundo.
Mujeres que no se conforman con vivir una
vida típica, siempre dejándose del hambre.

**You Are A Model for Women and Men
Rigoberta Menchú, Always Be the Way That You Are**

You are a strong woman ,
who in her thoughts of fighting
for la lucha, to help people, those
who are trying to defend their selves,

no matter if to reach it, they
have to lose their lives in la lucha
they think, and get a better place
to live, for them and for their next generations.

Rigoberta Menchú, in your form of help
you are not even thinking of getting married,
like all women dream, "Estoy abierta a la
vida"—You mean if you get married or not

it's not it for you. You only try
to help tu gente, that talks really good
of you. You are the woman. I like
your style.

                "Porque si no aprenden, no avanzan."
I agree with you. I have two years trying
to learn inglés as a second language,
it's not easy, but I worked for 6 years

in the fields. During these years I could
see that if you want to climb the
mountain, you have to work hard on
your life and never give up. "Todo

llega a su tiempo y cuando se
hace con calma es cuando las cosas marchan
bien," as you say it. It's the way
that I see it too, because after

six years that I couldn't study,
I have the opportunity to do it
again, and I try to do my
best everyday. Gracias,

Rigoberta Menchú. Gracias por qué
te preguntaras, gracias porque with your
story tú me diste fuerzas para
seguir through the hard way

that I have to walk every day.
Gracia muchas gracias, Rigoberta Menchú.

Dear Rosario Castellanos,
The Changes That You Made Rosario Castellanos,
The Changes for Women's Lives After You,
Rosario, Started Fighting For Them

After you, Rosario, started the changes with your
revolution for women, their lives changed in
economic, political and social ways.

After your revolution, for the women,
their lives changed economically.

      At this time in 1998, Yakima, the place
where I'm writing this letter, women
have "another way of being" than before. At
this time women can go to school, college,
even work for the same jobs, those that back in the
time, these were most of them for men. There
are men who still think that women are
for cleaning up the house and making some
tortillas, but, thanks to you, Rosario, of your
revolution for women. There are many women
who think that there has to be "another way of being
free and human" even for women.
Those women do as much as they can, to make
of this a better place to live their lives
with rights, where women can be what they
want to be.   After Rosario's revolution for women
their lives have changed socially.
      At this time women can feel
and educate their babies even without
the men's help. At this time the women don't
have to depend on the man anymore, like they
did back in the time. Is it not great, Rosario,
that something that you started—by writing
these beautiful poems, it's getting better every day.

After Rosario's revolution for women,

their lives changed politically.
                                  Thanks to Rosario
and her revolution,
the women have more rights than the rights
they had before. Women can vote
and give their own opinions to change the world.

This is how the world looks like at this time
for women's rights in Yakima, Washington.
Besos y abrazos querida Rosario, ójala que
te encuentras bien, donde quiera que estés.

Me hubiera gustado estar a tu lado,
para pelear juntos for the women's rights.

La Soledad

Estoy aquí solo y triste en mi soledad
porque el amor que quise

Ya no está
se fue, se fue

y nunca más volverá
En mi dejó una huella inmensa

Que jamás se borrará

Mi anhelo era tener tu cariño y tu amor
Pero lo que me queda es tu amargo calor

Tal vez era lo mejor para los dos
Tú no sabes mi verdadero dolor

Mi alma se perdió en lo más profundo del mar
Mi vida fue lo pasado, a pesar de tu engaño

Que triste es mi agonía
Desde tu viaje que hiciste aquella noche vida mía

Me encuentro muerto, pero en vida
Éste fue tu último poema querida.

Omar Ramírez Cruz

Siddhartha Eva

Siddhartha Eva Valdivia

My life is like a script of a divine play

I have a special glamour all my own

I am a splendorous light

I am sensitive and tolerant

I have knowledge of the unknown

I have old fashioned values

And my dreams become accomplishments

I am natural, emotional and considerate of others

I am powerful I am the enlightened one

My name means life I am Siddhartha

Rosa Permanente

Omar Ramíriz

My semblance
Rosa permanente
A bohemian
Bizarre wayfarer on the road without a course to follow
Disallowing a soul
Rosa permanente
Yo nací con un corazón de espinas debajo de la luna
A heart was converted into tears of tristeza
The discrepancy of the world and me
Isolated from your own bitter journey
Soy un extraño a su luz de infancia
A grief of souls
A lost life in abyss by the coast of *el olvido*
The word retarded kid
Will always be with me
I am like a thorn
Always attached to the rose of love
The bitter rose again
¿Por qué las rosas más hermosas siempre nacen con espinas amargas?

IV. Macchu Picchu

Don't let the boy die, let the man be stronger.

    Francisco

Going Up To Go Down: Mystical Journeys To Macchu Picchu

Queremos. Tenemos. Podemos.

We want to, and we can.

We choose because there is no choice.

We are sobrío, practical. Tenemos coraje.

We have ganas. Desire. Hunger. Even when cheapened by those who should know better, we have it, and we have it in quantity. Our ganas is our fuel. It's ok to be angry, too. We can use our anger. It can be converted into fuel. It must be, because there can be no anger in the heart. Not on this journey. We keep to our path. Our sendas. These are our impersonal principles. We do not need to take things personally. We only carry what we need in our mochilas and take out anything that we can't use. We are proud of our heridas. Our wounds.

These our the principios. Principios impersonales para ser abrecaminos.

Abrecaminos.

The way. The ways. To open the ways. To make a way where there is no way. Start where we are. And we're in different places. Start here.

To do this means we have to work on ourselves. Personal work. Inner work. The boy must become a man. Francisco writes a new refrane for us: Don't let the boy die, let the man be stronger. But some things must go. So we can get up this mountain. These are impersonal principles.

We listen to the women. That's a must. And to listen to them, really listen, to follow them when we need to follow, we have to do some work. Some inner work. Sube a nacer conmigo, hermano. We must leave some things behind.

Look inside. See where we've been hit. And sometimes not even aware of it. The little deaths. Daily ones. And bigger ones. Muertos graves.

The bullet and the bullet behind the bullet. Take the bullet and make a song. That's what goes on in these poems. Making music. Turning our lives into song.

Make a way where there is no way. We are chain breakers. Rompedores de cadenas. We keep to our path. Our paths. We are spiritual. Somos luchadores. Once we start we cannot go back.

There are guides. Hay guías. We can start over anytime we want. We are not inferior. Our response to what we've been given is all. We are hechos de oro.

We can get stuck. Estancado. Atrapado. No sabes para dónde ir. Ni que hacer. This is ok. This happens. We don't panic.

What are your metaphors? Identify them. It's easier for abrecaminos because the metaphors have been given to us earlier than for others.

Cross Rivers. Climb mountains.

Use the best from the past: dream dreams, see visions, speak in parables. But don't carry anything you don't need. Don't carry anything that makes it harder. It's hard enough as it is. Keep the dream. Leave no one behind. As a vision. Not everyone makes it.

Macchu Picchu is only a beginning. An arrival point. A departure point. Because on this journey, no one arrives. This is a way of no way. Cuando lleguemos. Nunca llegamos. But if we never arrive, we're always arriving. Home is here, in the way-making. It will be easier for others.

Jim Bodeen

Las Curvas de mi Vida

THE CURVES OF MY LIFE

Rubén Mendoza

I

It was 5:00 o'clock in the morning, I don't remember the day, but it was January, 1992. I was with my <u>abuelito</u> in the corral, feeding the cows and waiting for a newborn calf. It was still the early morning, and we were using flashlights to see. You could hear the <u>Grillos</u> jumping out of the bushes. After the calf was born, we went into the kitchen to eat breakfast. The smell was great, the <u>frijoles</u> were on the table, the <u>salsa</u> made in the <u>molcajete</u>, the <u>tortillas recién hechas</u> from the <u>comal</u> and the milk <u>recién ordeñada</u> from the cows. Before I sat down at the table, my grandmother called me from the <u>lavaderos</u>. I went as fast I could. When I got there I found my mother crying and my grandmother sitting on a rock, throwing little rocks to the cold water. Then

after a moment my grandmother told me that my mother was going away because she couldn't wait anymore for my father who was away from us because he was in this country.
I asked her why and she told me because she didn't want us anymore, neither me, my two sisters and my little brother. Then I began to cry and grabbed her dress, and she hit me in the mouth. She hit me so hard that I began to <u>sangrar</u>, and my grandmother hit her too. Then she went to the <u>troje</u>, and packed her personal things and told us bye, not for ever, but we were waiting for years and she never showed up. After that day my grandparents became our parents.

II

"I had no place to rest my hand"
       Pablo Neruda

I was playing with my little brother,
We were playing with our spinning top,
I was a beautiful day, on a Sunday afternoon.
When it was his turn to play,
He threw his spinning top,
He threw it so hard, that it hit me,
Right in my hand.
And I began to cry, because the pain was so powerful.
When I was at school, I couldn't write.
When I was at church, I couldn't move it.
Then after days of pain,
My brother told me, would you shut up!
You're a chicken! Coyón!

III

"Little death, events from one to eight"
       —Pablo Neruda

Every time I went to Uruapan,
The city that is near to my town,
I had to buy comics.
There was no day, that I wouldn't buy comics.
It was like a bad habit.
And from that day on, I just bought good books,

Like poetry books, mystery books or dictionaries,
I just read comics, when I don't have to buy them.

IV

"My friend the death"
   —Pablo Neruda

Who's this death?
Many people ask themselves that question.
For many people, the death is a bad guy,
La calaca, la huesuda, la pelona, la dientona, la mamona,
Who enjoys taking people to the other world, to her world.
For me the death, is a beautiful woman,
The most beautiful woman I ever seen.
The lady who talks, and stands by my side,
When time I need her.
When she gets to our place,
Un viento helado sopla contra mi cara,
Y un sudor frío recorre todo mi cuerpo.
Pero no por mucho tiempo,
Porque ella está ahí para quitarme el frío,
Con amor y sentimiento.
Para mí ella lo es todo,
Todo lo que puedo imaginar,
Mi amiga, mi vida, mi esposa y mi amante.
Cuando ella está conmigo,
No me siento nervioso,
Porque ella me hace olvidar todo.

V

"An atom from the breast,
that did not come to the combat"
   —Pablo Neruda

I was a coward at that time,
even death was making a fool of me,
But like the rabbit,

My soul jumped on her with frenzy.
I hit death with me *resortera*,
When my mother went away,
I killed the rabbits,
And took them out of their misery.

VI

"Madre de piedra espuma de los condores"
    —Pablo Neruda

Madre de piedra,
Espuma de los cóndores,
Como la brisa del mar,
Que llega hasta lo alto,
De las altas montañas.
Machu Pichu, hija del sol,
Que hasta los reyes,
Del más poderoso imperio,
Se hincan ante tu esplendor.
De tus benditas enternas,

Fuego que ha de quemar,
Los pecados de tus hijos,
Y de los hijos de tus hijos.
Maldito el que se atreva,
A quebrantar tus leyes,
A violar tu virginidad y pureza,
Porque el fuego de tus entrañas,
Lo devora al inofensivo conejo.

VII

"Sube conmigo amor americano"
    —Pablo Neruda

Sube conmigo amor americano,
Que llegarémos hasta el universo,
Mientras escalamos la montaña,

Las piedras rodarán hasta el abismo.
Fronteras que no han podido separarnos,
Tal vez porque somos invencibles,
O tal vez porque no han podido envenenarnos.
Cruzaremos los ríos más largos,
Los más anchos o caudalosos,
Pero nunca cruzaremos los ríos, por donde corre la sangre,
Sangre de los caídos en guerras inútiles,
Guerras que se pelean entre los gobiernos hipócritas.
No importa si comienza la tercerea guerra mundíal,
O si se acerca el fin del mundo,
Porque después de la muerte,
Volveremos a estar juntos.

VIII

"Tiempo en el tiempo, el hombre, dónde estuvo?"
 —Pablo Neruda

I want to know, why am I taking this class?
I want to know, why should I do this poem?
I want to know, why am I coming to school?
I want to know, why I came to this country?
I want to know, why am I still here?
I want to know everything!
Could you give me an answer?
Answer me!
Don't just stand there like a *venado* who is afraid of me!
Maybe the *pizarrón* will answer me?
Or maybe the *mesabancos*?
Should I ask the computer?
Or should I ask the floor?
May be I should ask myself?
Then, after years of asking, may be...?

IX

"Déjame olvidar, ancha piedra, la proporción poderosa"
—Pablo Neruda

Let me forget, great stone,
The powerful proportion,
Let me forget, the bad things of my life,
Let me forget, the baseness of the men!
And let me remember the good things I have lived.
Because, maybe when I'll have to be in hell,
I will remember the day, my mother left us,
And I remember it, with powerful pain,
Pain that every day hits and destroys my brain.
I also remember the day,
I met my father again,
And I remember it, like the most wonderful day of my life.
But I have no confidence,
That always will be that way,
May be my life will change its course,
Like the river changes its direction.

X

"Rise up to be born with me, my brother"
—Pablo Neruda

We are climbing the mountain.
With out fear, with out scaring each other,
Because we are brothers and sisters,
And nothing else matters, just you and me.
Here we are in school,
In class, reading these poems,
With our friends waiting for graduation,
It doesn't matter the color of your skin,
Or the place you were born,
If you are white, black American, native American,
Hispanic or even if the color of your skin is red.
That's why we're getting to the top of the mountain,
Because, we care for each other,

Like the mother cares for her child.

Adiós a Mi Niñez

Javier Vargas

I

Surrounded by those who don't get along,
by dehydrated flowers.
I'm in a sad world, which loses life.
Surrounded by those who live in death
and hold on to luck,
unique people, afraid to salute.
My skin is accepted and rejected
in a strange place, distant from my roots,
where sweating heavens
and bleeding rivers help apples mature.
I walk through everyone's land,
through the streets of the future.
I walk without fear,
I walk with fear,
I walk with confidence,
Sometimes I get lost.
I live exploring the world,
oh, how difficult the world is!
I live with light

and the shadows are near.
I live with full and heavy days,

with black heavens accompanied by hopes.

II

Another cold beginning,
another day to live.
One more opportunity to learn,
another way to release the pain and keep on going.
How many stars will be turned off
and how many will be born tonight?
How many roots will starve?
when will we all wake up and realize
What we do to mother earth?
We beat her instead of protect and caress her.
France and others
with their nuclear tests,
idolizing radiation,
the United States
increasing discrimination.
Cancer,
multiplying in more women's breasts,

AIDS, without fear, without censorship.
Where are we going?
Are we going somewhere or nowhere?

III

Life is full of dangers,
        ¿Qué se puede hacer?
We don't take action,
        sólo sabemos perder.

Losing our planet
        es cada día más un hecho,
but why do we let that happen?
        No tendremos ningún derecho!
We segregate
        en lugar de trabajar en grupo,
What is the cause of that?
        ¡yo que sé, nadie supo!
We blame each other
        como perros peleando por huesos,
We seem to be tarugos,
        gente que no utiliza los Cesos.
We're capable of uniting
        permanentemente nuestras razas,
but when talking about it
        cada quien para su casa.
We are afraid
        de conocer lo desconocido,
        de sentir que al explorar
        nos siéntamos perdidos.
We have strength
        pero casi nunca lo utilizamos,
we want to run
        pero tenemos los pies hundidos en pantanos.
Together
        somos la agrupación perfecta,
Let's walk hand with hand
        hasta el final de nuestras metas.
We are billions of worlds on top of
        un solo mundo,

we're killing it,
        desde el exterior hasta lo profundo.
¡Let's do something caramba!
        ¡Despierten con una fregada!
If we fail once
        ¿Qué perdemos? ¡Nada!

IV

Two and a half years were your life,
little one,
tanned skin,
prietita.
Girl with curls made by *mamá*,
tender beauty.
How would you be like today?
you'll turn fifteen in paradise,
you're gone.
I still don't let go of you,
I'll never let go of you.
I know that every night and always
you are our family's guardian angel.
Water is life,
water took one of your lives,
now you live in heaven, my dear sister.
Why do we have to die?
It is not enough to live and consume time
for a decomposing ending,
there has to be something else, right?
Life is to be born and more,
and to be born is death sentence.

V

To death:
Get the hell out of my path!
I don't want you around me,
I want to go to college!
Who the hell do you think you are, huh?!
Don't you understand that I want to get married some day
and be happy for a while?
Leave me alone!
I don't want you in my neighborhood.
I don't fear you, I just detest you!
Don't you have something better to do Mrs. Death?
Do you enjoy watching us kill each other?

Why don't you knock,
Why do you take without asking?
I respect you,
but you have to respect me,
you have to respect my dreams,
you have to feel life
to understand why I deny you.
I'll see you later Mrs. Death,
when I feel like I'm ready to go with you,

NOT NOW.

VI

     Sé que poco a poco se consiguen las cosas,
que uno se cae para levantarse con más fuerzas.
En todo camino hay piedras con que tropezarse
y espinas que se clavan en los pies,
en el corazón, en el alma.
Si te dejas, todo se te viene encima,
pero si decides continuar sin miedo,
el mundo es tuyo, todo es tuyo.
Sueños, esperanzas, metas, amor,
son parte de la vida,
también hay tristezas, decepciones,
     hay de todo para todos.
Hay veces que te hace falta expresar lo que sientes,
si no lo haces, te ahogas.
Hay que ver la luz,
     las flores,
cosas positivas que la tierra
y todo lo espiritual tienen que ofrecernos.
Hay que ser fuerte
y chillar cuando tengamos que hacerlo.
Hay que amar la vida,
aunque te parta el alma por un rato.

VII

Este poema es para usted, madre.
                Mujer mexicana,
                Hecha y derecha,
                mujer fiel a su familia,
mi chaparrita, prietita de Guerrero,
la que sabe luchar por lo que quiere.
Usted nos ha dado de comer y beber,
sin usted no supiéramos que hacer.
Gracias por cargarnos en su fuerte vientre
por tantos meses,
y criarnos por tantos años.
Gracias por confiar en mi, su hijo mayor.
No tengo malos vicios,
        ¿Por qué?
Por usted jefecita,
porque la amo,
porque la respeto y me respeto,
porque quiero lo mejor para usted,
así como usted quiere lo mejor para mí.
Gracias por sus sacrificios,
        Por perdonar los enojos que le he hecho pasar.
Me siento orgulloso de ser su hijo.
Mujer trabajadora, ejemplar como ninguna.
"La quiero mucho Amá."

VIII

Que lejos estoy de ti
        tierra extrañada,
amada por muchos,
por otros desgraciadament olvidada.
Mírame aquí buscándome a mí mismo,
no te puedo ver,
no te puedo tocar,
pero te puedo recordar.
yo te amo lugar bendito,

cuando me ahogo en las aguas del recuerdo,
te grito.
Vives conmigo,
soy tu amigo.
Te llevo en mis pasos,
pues de tu riqueza soy heredero,
quiero volver a ti,
quiero mirar tus cielos,
quiero besar tu tierra,
quiero que me perdones por haberte abandonado,
quiero ver a mis abuelos,
quiero ser un niño otra vez
y jugar bajo tus lluvias,
correr descalzo por las calles de mi pueblo.

IX

Without the lights
I would be the blindest of the blind.
I wouldn't see the injustice.
I would turn my back to the truth,
I would be in an infernal place.
Without the plants,
I wouldn't know the meaning of: Colors.
Without the rain,
I wouldn't understand my tears.
Without the sun,
there would be no hell and no life.
Without the earth,
my ancestors could not have created me.
my character would be weak,
Without dreams,
I would be a spider web, sinking in water,
an eye without pupil,
dry water or painted wind.
Without my family,
the snow would burn me.
Without deceptions, my heart wouldn't break,

Without my indigenous blood,

my eyes would be nothing but abandoned tunnels.

X

No sé quien serás, pero te encontraré,

Te voy a amar, serás mía, te seré fiel.

Desnudos descubriremos el pecado,

nuestros cuerpos se comerán cada vez que hagamos el amor.

Amaré tus ojos, tu espíritu, tu pelo, tus senos,

tus músculos, tu cuerpo entero.

Besaré. lameré y acariciaré tu piel mm^2 xmm^2,

desde las puntas de tus pies hasta las puntas de tu pelo.

No te ofreceré lo que no sea mío,

ni dinero, ni el cielo, ni la luna, ninguna estrella,

te ofreceré mi amor, mujer bella.

Voy a conocerte, tus labios morderte.

Cada noche cenaré de tu boca,

te haré el amor hasta que te sientas loca.

Viviremos en un pequeño nido, lleno de amor y comprensión,

entre nosotros habrá comunicación.

Seremos aves volando y jugando en pleno vuelo.

¿Sabes? me hace falta alguien con quien

compartir mis alegrías y montones de penas,

alguien en quien refugiarme de este mundo hipócrita,

alguien que me mire a los ojos

y me diga: "te creo."

Ese alguien serás tú, mi futura esposa,

serás de mi vida la Diosa.

No te quiero perfecta, yo no soy perfecto.

Mi corazoncito y yo te estaremos buscando y esperando,
estaremos pendientes, con nuestras manos abiertas
                              Hasta luego

XI

To life:

Hit me harder if you want,
Kick my mouth if you want,
Knock me down and bury me with stones if you want
I'm ready to destroy your walls.
I see you complete and lasting, life.
Your walls will be unknown pains,
but I'm strong, I can deal with them.
You might slap or spit my face,
but you will not kill what I am,
I know you wouldn't even think of killing me, life.
I'm not that little boy
with sad facial expressions anymore.
I'm saying good bye to my childhood,
the sad boy will be behind
but always with me.

I'm not going to erase anything,
all will be recorded in my senses.
I'm going to utilize every second you give me,

LIFE.

XII

I'm discovering myself,
risking everything on a new road,
learning the meaning of walking on this world.
I'm growing, I feel more mature.
I see clarity and darkness in my path,
I don't see evil covering my eyes.
I see struggles in my path,
dreams that become reality.
I don't see demons.
I see love, my own family.

    Not everything I see is beautiful,

    Not everything I see is horrible.

I see the land and its seas in my hands,

I see the universe reserving a place for me.

There's so much left for me to live.

My future will not be decided by any more but me.
Not even God can tell me what I should do,
I'm going to enjoy seeing
how those who lie about me bite their tongues.

I will keep walking eternally,
even after my so called "death."
I will do what no one has done,
I will help with what I can,
I will see what no one has seen,

I will say what no one wants to talk about,

I will fight against injustice,

I'm going to change the world. (it could happen).

Exiting the Old, To Arrive Into the New

Angel Ayon

I
"Someone awaiting me among the violins discovered a world like an entombed tower."

I can see my dad's warm face.
His proud smile and opened arms.
I know through his experiences in life,
I need to work hard.
The Strength he passes on to me through his warm embrace.
He waits for me each day when I get home to ask how
my day went. He is a sensitive man.
But rough and rigid also.
I thank that all that I have in him.
I am so grateful.
God, I know anyone would wish to have the parents I do.
To receive all the love I get everyday.
I am so lucky and grateful.
Thank you God for blessing with this wonderful life.

II
"that I touched before on stone or in the lightning unleashed by a kiss"

I know this feeling. I've felt it before.
When I look into your eyes I see a past that
I once knew. I see a boy and girl who share a deep love.
It's all coming back too clear. Do I want it to surface?
Maybe, maybe not. But it feels good.
I like to have your moist lips kiss my forehead. I like
how I can trust you. I'm not embarrassed to act
dumb around you. And sometimes when you act dumb
also we stop and laugh at each other together.
I know this feeling. I've felt it before.
You're different though. Your ways are
new. New things and changes are good.
Good for my soul. You are both.

So what can I do to keep you.
What can we do to keep each other.
We must open our eyes and our hearts and see and feel
what really lies there. Don't be afraid.
Shine through.

III
"Anything that hurts the spirit is a little death"

So you thought I could never escape.
You never thought I would be able to free myself of your grasp.

That grasp of yours that brought me down.
It made me a lesser person inside.
So what can I do to keep you.
What can we do to keep each other.
We must open our eyes and our hearts and see and feel
what really lies there. Don't be afraid.
Shine through.

III
"Anything that hurts the spirit is a little death"

So you thought I could never escape.
You never thought I would be able to free myself of your grasp.

That grasp of yours that brought me down.
It made me a lesser person inside.

I felt like I wasn't wanted.
I killed you though.

With small blows I erased you.
You no longer hide in the crevices of my heart.

I no longer fear you.
With the little death of you, a spirit was born inside of me.

A spirit that shows through the things I do. How I treat you.
How I treat myself.

IV
"Mighty death invited me many times:
It was like invisible salt in the waves"

I have been invited to die my death many times. The times I went to
parties with the girls and drank, drank to have more fun.
The guys were all around staring at each girl and waiting to see
which one would give it up the quickest.
Maybe I would be tipsy enough to just walk into
that back room with him.
The lights dim and the music blaring.
The music seems to echo off the walls of this tiny house.
The girls whisper about each other and laugh to their friends.
A potential fight waiting to happen.
I drank because I liked the way I felt.
I liked being able to act any way I wanted and have it be O.K.
Everyone knew I had the alcohol in my system.
Then, its time to go. I offer to drive.
I didn't know what I was doing. I'm always in control.
Not then, Not when I let those around me make my decisions for me.
I drove and the whole while I thought these dreams were so real.
My god guided me those times. He must have a plan for me
because I was not called to join him them.
I want to tell these other girls a thing or two.
Yeah, you're bad. But , remember
there's always somebody badder and tougher.
You think you're the only one who's been to juvi. Look around.
Open your eyes.
The person you'd most likely think has nothing to worry about,
has already been there and back.
Still I died those times. I was killed.
Yet, I kept going back. The curiosity of just how far I could go.
Then like a snap of a finger.
My innocence as a child died.
It was trampled on.
The life squeezed out—pain.

Like a lost kid searching for its mother,
I searched and searched for the woman in me and found her.

V
"and in the world I found nothing but a chilling gust"

As I drive down the road, I pass a man who's car has broken down.
I don't stop to help because I'm scared.

Although I have a brand new pair of jumpers in my trunk.
Who can I trust?

I can't trust anyone.

Like the gay student who was murdered, nobody helped him,
they simply didn't know him.

If we can't trust each other, than what?
What makes you think you can even trust yourself?

I hear these stories and through experiences of my own, I'm appalled.
I'm disgusted by the way our society works.
By the way I work.

We're closing our eyes to the needy and looking the other way.
But, how can we change? We are killing ourselves
and dying a long slow death.

VI
"until they recognized them in the night or in death"

I remember years ago,
when there was a huge void in the family.
It wasn't how it was supposed to be.
I could see the hurt in my dad's smile.
That day was my aunt's funeral.
My dad's sister. My aunt.
Her beautiful face all done in too much makeup.

Her hair exquisitely curled, although I don't ever remember
it being that way.
That was a day the gap seemed to close a little.
Everyone pulled together then.
But as I think and wonder, why a death?
Why does something so tragic and horrible
have to be the means of reconciling?
Isn't love greater than hate?
Sometimes, It takes one person to say sorry,
and like a chain reaction everyone follows?
So why wait for a death like my family did.
It only brings more tears.
I think it's God's way of showing us that something good
also comes out of something bad.
It has to be.
That day as my uncles and aunts became brothers and sisters again,
I realized the distance life goes to make a change or to prove a point.

VII
"all that you were has fallen: customs, frayed syllables,
masks of dazzling light."

The way I feel now, is the real me.
When I first walked into the door of this class,
I found a man with curly ash blond hair, who had
a knowing smile on his face.
His eyes looked right through me and I knew that
I would enjoy this class.
I thought I knew who I was.
I knew who I wanted to be.
My teacher guided me to bring out the hardships
love wants, and desires, on paper.
Slowly I began to realize what my inner self looked like.
Like so many others,
I want to be better.
The ways I had, have changed.
And the best feeling through all this is knowing
that I did it myself.
I make up my mind. I make up my own world.

VIII
"innocence is always yours, it's the innocence that's born
when the lie dies" Mr. Bodeen

The weekend went all too quick
I was there at the party dancing.
My feet and arms moving quick to the beat,
I have learned, I don't need alcohol to have a good time.
So when it was offered, I didn't drink.
The night played on.
My hair wet and straight from the sweat.
The sweat I had generated from getting down on the dance floor.
The closeness I felt towards him intensified.
The way he held me in his arms during the slow songs.
The way I felt made me close my eyes and feel complete.
The dance soon faded into tomorrow.
I was relieved to go. Where was I going? We had other plans.
The whole night I felt God's presence.
I felt the way I did when he was with me last time. God.
The chills I get, the energy ready to explode.
All the love in the world seemed to be in my hands.
We snuck out quietly getting into my car,
He kissed me the whole while.
His lips are always warm against mine.
We drove to a dark spot.
Our kisses more hot and heavy.
The way two curious children are at play, we didn't hesitate.
Our clothes seemed to find their way off onto the floor.
I felt him close to me. Almost in me,
then a bright light. Hurry, Hurry,
in a rush the clothes went back in their place.
Was it a sign?
Was it God telling me no.
Telling me, yelling at me,
"No, mija, don't not yet"
It was—for then, we went home and only a trace of kisses he left on me.
And not the traces of his man being.
The next day. He told me something.
Oh how my throat tightens and my voice breaks at the thought.
He told me no that night. He told me to wait.

He has chlymidia.
He went to get tested for AIDS.
My whole dreams and life could have been swept under my feet.
He said he wanted to get checked first.
Does this change my love for him?
No, love is unconditional.
I love him for who and what he is.
I thanked him for waiting.
I thanked him for not putting me in danger. In jeopardy.
I thanked and am still thanking God.
But what if, in two weeks, the tests come back positive?
What am I to do?
Am I to say good-bye and give one last kiss.
He asked me, What if?
I laughed and told him, I'm here.
I am here to go through this together with him.
Love is about happiness.
Love is about being with God.
I know God is with me. I pray to you Lord Jesus to be with him also.
Maybe barely now, I've found my mountain.
These two weeks of waiting, waiting to see if my love
is unconditional, is ironic.
"Like walking barefoot on knife-sharp rocks"
is what Jerry said. I feel this way now.

IX

soft home
silver silence
rocks
delicious music
chattering bed
vision

green family
excited hair
messy prayer
strong running
silky school

rocky silk
                innocent

losing clock
                prickly

        naked cat

laughing illusions
sunken rose

                                                        rose shoes

X

I want to know what the garden feels.
I want to know how to open doors.
I want to know how hot the fire really is.
I want to know what is on the other side of my mirror.

Tell me how nail polish is made.
Tell me what I look like.
Tell me your innermost secret of life.
Tell me how much you love me and want me.

XI

I see a dark cloud after the rain fading in the sky.
I see my people growing old under the porch light.
I see a little boy crying alligator tears.
I do not see the thorn in the rose.
I do not see my feet.
I see these pencil marks on paper that leave me naked
in the light for everyone to see.
I see the ink in my pen slowly getting used up.
I do not see what color socks you're wearing.
"You are a voice for those who don't have voices."

XII

These changes I've went through are powerful.
I look into the light and see my face.

I am powerful. I am strong.
I am a beautiful young woman and am not afraid of the world.

I know my struggles. I do not know my future.
Half of my journey is already over.

My life is always changing.
My views are different each day.

I'm sure of the person I can be.
My power is my ability to take all of my

experiences and knowledge and change myself.
I am changing myself into that person.

My strength comes from all of you around me.
It comes from the struggles everyday
that you and me together have overcome.

Acid Silence

Juan Ortega

I.

"... *acid silence.*"
   —Pablo Neruda.

The loudest noise in the world.
Ruido. Our pal that keeps us from thinking straight.
Thinking the truth.
One gasps for sound,
like one gasps for air.
Aguas. It's Silent Reading Time. SRT.
Twenty of the scariest minutes I can think of.
Good thing the desks face one direction.
If not, people might try to have eye contact with you,
and try to communicate. Silently.
Don't let me remember.

I know. I'll draw something.
Nothing meaningful, just something to exchange
for this loud absence.
When the birds begin to sing and SRT is over,
my closed fists relax, I breathe again.

I leave reality for a minute.
Everything is out of place. Who are you?
The board reads "Mr. Bodeen".
Boy, this guy really stands out. Then again so do I.
Even though, I feel I'm supposed to be here.

Behind him there's a fight going on.
Blood splatters clear to my desk in the middle of the room,
staining my avocado colored shirt.
I didn't like it anyway. *El color da asco.*
The bloody scene engulfs the students attention,
like a tornado engulfs Scottbluff, Nebraska.
People cheer as the Aztec finishes off the iron clothed Spaniard.
But the damage was done.
The "triumphant" Aztec slowly died in front of our eyes.
I look around the room at my Mexican compañeros.
All with their catholic crosses in hand.

II.

"*. . . without a dagger?*"
  —Pablo Neruda.

I pass a man sitting gracefully on the curb,
making love to his sandwich.
His looks up at me and mumbles,
"Daggers are useful! Be sure to get your own."
I think to myself,
"What the hell? Get this guy his shot of whisky."

Many, in life, struggle to get a direction.
A cause. A dagger.
Bees have their beehive to worry about.

Lions have their pride to worry about.
Catholics have heaven and hell to worry about.
Mexicans have breakfast to worry about.
Mothers have lots of shit to worry about.
And you? What's the dagger that's killing you?
Saving you!

"Sein oder nicht sein. Dass ist die frage"
Sounds much better in German. Don't you think?
Especially when it's foreign.

Get a dagger.
Get one before the good ones are taken.
Because without one,
someone might as well read that eulogy

III.

"... *rodent of the teeming streets.*"
        —Pablo Neruda.

Where to go? What to do?
It's dark! Wet.
I haven't seen any of those big hairless rodents.
I wonder how they stand up straight like that.
I hope I never have to stand that high (that arrogant).

Hey, there goes that rodent I saw yesterday.
The one with the shiny fur and pretty tail.
Maybe she'll share my cheese with me.
Perhaps she'll carve a hole in the wall with me.
Or she might just spit on me.
Fifty, fifty. That's good enough for me .

Oooh! Check it out!
It's one of those Mickey Mouse watches.
Mick's not tickin'.
It figures. All talk and no show.
What does he have that I don't.

Besides a zillion dollar contract with Disney.
I'm not so sure I'd want to be that stinkin' rich.
After a while, it's hard to tell the nice one from the bitch.

No thanks! I'll just sit here with the rest of the losers
and eat my government cheese.

IV.

"... *nocturnal clarity.*"
  —Pablo Neruda.

Swooping down from your racing chariot in the sky,
better than Batman does,
you retrieve for your victim
like a spider retrieves a tangled fly.
You go undisturbed in your mission.
Your mission to take the most valuable given.
Some call you *Díablo,* some *Teufel,* some Devil,
and others, *Power*.

Power to strike fear in most,
and relief in some.
Fear in O.J. Simpson. Not of death, but of no life.

You give us closure, and then rebirth.
You thrive in oil slick roads of racing cars,
deep in the branches of bare trees in Autumn.
I can imagine you die too. In your own way(s).

No one quits life, one just exchanges it for something else.
It's up to that three pound mass,
in one's skull, to decide what you're exchanging.
Some people/things don't give a shit.
I do. I want my Complimentary Refill.
I'm not afraid!

V.

"*. . . the breast that did not come to combat.*"
    —Pablo Neruda.

went to the orchards to help pick apples.
For it couldn't do much else,
except for love.
Love everything in its path.
The mask that clothed it,
the soap that cleans it,
the hand that caresses it.

Its own beauty is enough for it.
Its world does not exceed the size of the room.
What it must feel like to be so simple, so beautiful.

VI.

"*In you, as in two parallel lines. . .*"
    —Pablo Neruda.

your amazement feeds the hunger of curiosity,
and your love of women burns holes in your skull.

Take a bite of the other half of the sandwich.
Taste that of which you have not seen, yet.
Du musst mehr hunger haben!
I suppose you've never wondered about
the science that makes the solar system,
that makes cream-filled popsicles,
that makes you and I(i).
Those limitations bury us like chewed dog bones.
No arms. No legs to set us *libre*.
Libre to walk around in ectoplasmic computers.

Those flat feet of ours
are the frontiers of everything we do.
Leave that pencil-shaped country of yours
and push back those frontiers.

push them back so far that the cuticles of your fingers
bleed that sacred Indian blood.
Burn those Indian huts and villages,
but take pictures first,
because it's so important to
remember the leather-like skin
half our ancestors had.
If not for Columbus, Cortés, Amerigo, and the rest,
we would be much more different.
Their curiosity shaped the polygonal
lives that are yours and mine.

VII.

*"When the clay-colored hand turned to clay,
when the little eyelids closed."*
  —Pablo Neruda

My subconscious awakened
like the gentle beast it is.
Dreaming of the country-side Autobahns.
Inhabiting German engineering that make those cars
drag race with the wind.
The narrow chair I sit in cramps my muscles,
and the cold ventilation makes my jaw weak.
I raise my weary arm to twist close
this wicked annoyance.
The low whistle of the 747
hushes the passengers and most go to sleep.
Below, the dark majestic abyss rumbles.

Now the gliding mass braces
for a rubber screeching halt.
A single bell announces
that yellow teethed smokers discontinue
their own distruction for about two minutes.
The over weight man next to me
manages to get his seat-belt on.

He closes his eyes.
I imagine him thinking of
his wife, his dog, his BMW.
The most beautiful scenery is observed from the
open heavens.
I always feel sorry for the sap who
paid thousands and asked for a window
only to sit above the enormous wings.

Here I am.
A strangely exciting place.
A place to fall in love with
and fall in love at.
My journey isn't over.

VIII.

"The dead kingdom is still alive."
  —Pablo Neruda.

Its heart pulsates
with blood, thousand of years old.
A kingdom of bright invisibility.
Open your eyes and see,
the Nazi-like rage this kingdom has.
Open your eyes and see
it hiding like a coward behind
its castle.
Castle of ignorance surrounded
by a moat of stupidity.
Open your eyes and see,
religion sewing your
eyes and mouth shut.
Open your eyes and see,
the members of this society.
They're everywhere.
They're your neighbors,
your judges, your cops,

your teachers, your friends.

Join me and we'll exorcize
this demon kingdom.

IX.

"Granite lamp, stone bread."
  —Pablo Neruda.

Crumpled memories.
Shiny backboard.
Dirty crown.
Rounded pills.
Frowning clouds
Screeching oilslicks.
Thorny women.
Excited chair.
Flat keys.
Jagged plateaus.
Folded iron.

X.

*". . . did you too store in the depths of your bitter intestine,
  like an eagle, hunger."*
  —Pablo Neruda.

I thrive in the security that is mine
and only mine.
For me, any obscurity is my death.
Look at me! Do what I do.
For there's no choice.
No freedom to rearrange
this shelf of wisdom so often misused.
I want to know what you know.
(What everyone knows!)
I want to know what's beyond.
Beyond the blue walls of oxygen.

I want to know how it's done.
How all has become private. Sacred.
I want to know existence here is
more than physical.

Tell me the secret which opens
the door to eternal power.
Tell me where you come from,
where you live, what you eat,
how you travel within everyone.

XI.

"I see a body, a thousand bodies, a man, a thousand women. . ."
  —Pablo Neruda

All of them, as valuable as the gold
they were made of.
Mothers, sisters, aunts and grandmas.
All left behind and equal.
I see the way men are.
And I say, "Why?"
Why has the universe done such
a thing to women?
I see the atrocities society(ies),
have burdened women with.
I don't see equality.
Make it fair someone.
Make it fun more often.

Have the world smile simultaneously.

XII.

"Your stiff voice will not return."
  —Pablo Neruda.

¡Carnal!
Where did you go?
Your absence chokes the life from my happiness,
like a dog chokes on chicken bones.
Happiness that for 17 years has been dulled to a sandy haze.
All those moments when I needed a brother,
you......You were busy becoming Lt. Dan Taylor.
At times, I thought hard to recall your existence,
but my hazy memory failed me.
I received a much anticipated letter from you,
or better yet, your secretary.
When you called, you spoke an eternity with Mamá,
and a minute to me.
I no longer knew what to say to you.
A 747 reunited us, only to become more distant.
I never knew how "indifference" could hurt.
I hope someday I can speak to you as a true brother,
not a biological half-brother

V. Short Stories

"¿Qué demonios era éso? asked his grandma. She turned to look outside. He made eye contact with her and waved. She waved back and signaled to him to go to the front door. There was his grandma standing in the doorway…

The World

Citlamina Caltenco

It's hard to see the world. I want to get "new" eyes and better glasses. Maybe I'll see it.

"Why am I blaming myself?"

"THEY." The world needs to get new eyes and better glasses.

I know who I am and where I come from, I know my struggles and especially my strength. I know what I want.

Still. I'm barely learning how to break some of the walls that have been put up by my own raza.

"Can't they see that it hurts...We work, we sweat, we see the sunrise and most important we know who we are."

I love myself. I love my family. And those who work in the

same office as I do. The office where we get to feel nature, see it, and be in a partnership with it.

I ask one more time, "Can't they see me? Can't they see us?"

I guess not because they don't know our stories or our office.

I know I'm a liberal, I want to explore, and I want to teach others. That's why you should stop by my office and feel our stories.

I hear the keyboard click. The fan. The chairs squeak when someone moves. It's quiet. Then noise comes into my world, and I realize that it's Monday in Latino Literature class. I'm supposed to be writing, but I look at a book in front of me and instead I want to LISTEN. I think that will become a better story.

Guadalajara

I didn't know where I was going. All I knew was that I was going to get to see my father after…well, I can't remember. I had Chicken Pox. My mother took all three of us to Guadalajara to get our Visa.

My brother had gotten over the Chicken Pox because he was the one who got them first. Now my sister and I had them. We camped out right in front of the building, I remember. I remember. That's one of the few things that I remember very clearly. I was the one whining the most. My brother tried to help my mom but I could see the pain and frustration in my mother's face.

My mother said we were lucky to be that close. I remember, the line was so long, at least two blocks ahead of us.

We had blankets, the morning was cold. I was hungry and those Chicken Pox! My sister and I had a fever of 103 degrees. My mom kept on saying that they would open soon. But we were four to five hours early.

Finally, when that time came, my mom got worried because she had to leave us outside. She didn't know what to say or even what to expect.

My brother gave us the medicine, and held me in his arms. I was only seven I think. I cried for a little time. I was confused. I really didn't know what was going on. Now I realize that that pain is still with me, and that memory will always be there too.

That's a normal day for Guadalajara's Visa Department. I'm sure a lot of other people go through a lot worse, but nobody knows their stories. There are many days to come and a lot more people to gather at that spot so early in the morning.

The Bed

My body is stuck to the bed. My father shakes me from the shoulders, saying, "Come on, Lazy, are you going to come or not, because I'm leaving in 15 minutes."

I'm half-way asleep and answer, "No sé, Tengo mucha flojera."

"You know you'll have more money to take to México this summer…Come on, get up!"

My mind gets going and I know I have to get the energy from somewhere. A great guilt overwhelms my body. I say to myself, "I have to go, my dad is counting on me, I'm his partner."

The silence in the house gives me an idea of how early it is.

I get up.

Get dressed.

Eat.

Brush my teeth.

And grab our lunch.

And right before I open the door I see my father yawn, and I realize that he is tired, too.

> The mornings; cold and silent.
> The afternoons; hot and tiring.
> Summer.

I worship those early mornings and afternoons working with my father. I know that our relationship is getting where I want it to be.

Dreams

My dreams are so real. I was there watching myself make the same mistake over and over.

My head hurts.

I know somebody is watching, but I don't know that it's me. I felt the presence of myself.

I watched everything that I was doing.

I was in bed dreaming, what I'm telling you now.

There was a blue sky and then….

I go back to my dream about myself.

Suddenly I remember Ms. Gunderson. That smell in her room, that no one else has. The excitement in her face when she's talking….I remember, she was trying to get her point across.

The incense, the candles, perfume, and the lotion make that relaxing smell in her room.

Oh, let's not forget the coffee.

As she walks into class she starts talking about the latest news and at the same time she's getting ready to brew coffee.

That coffee that makes "them" happy.

That noise that makes me happy. And the smell that reminds me of all the Folger's commercials.

Drip drip and a soft echoing crunching sound. The coffee is brewing.

No more drips, only the echoing crushing sound for about a minute and a half. Then silence, only a long drip that lasts until the coffee pot is full.

Those drips keep me from dreaming.

I watch her.

Then I dream. The drip of the coffee brewing. It's a constant repetition for 100 minutes.

Then I realize there is a connection between the blue sky and her. She always says that there will be two moons or suns, but that one of them will be blue.

"I wish I could know everything," I say to myself. Saying it with the frustration that I don't know half of the vocabulary that the rest of the IB (International Baccalaureate/college bound) English students know.

Looking down at my Commentary Score I see a "2" and right away I know it's the language part.

Forgetting about my grade I look at Jessie, who says, "I wore yellow that day. That's why I got all "5's."

Ms. Gunderson comes into my head again. You know...I agree with the girl that read that night. In Poetry Night. Here at Davis."

I remember that night. I was there for my own good. I wanted to know what it was.

As she went to the podium I asked myself, "Why didn't I come these three years?"

Then...AAU—! comes into my head, as the girl says it with joy.

I didn't know what she was talking about, because I ignored everything before that.

I was slowly and quietly searching for the answer to my question.

She made everybody laugh, and suddenly I caught myself thinking that this was one of the best days that I've had here at Davis.

As my boyfriend and I listen to her love poem, we both blindly search for each other's hand as if we knew what she was talking about.

We both listen closer to the words, and then….He laughs. I look at him and he says nothing. I go back to the reader and let go of his hand.

Then I watch her eyes.

They look at Ms. Gunderson. And she speaks. "Ms. Gunderson, you are the Fifth Element."

I smile and agree with what she says.

Gundi smiles too, appreciating her comment.

The girl finishes her poem and I catch myself dreaming again.

My first English teacher in high school.

Who, by the way, I said HI to when I came in.

Cooper is now in my sight. I remember that I have to go home and read Pedro Páramo for his class tomorrow.

The responsibility grew stronger. I had already made eye contact with him.

Remembering a Friend

Salvador Castañeda Muñiz

It was almost dark. I was visiting a friend who lived one block away from my house. Everyone in our neighborhood knew each other pretty well. I was visiting my friend Edgar when one of my other friends came by and wanted me to go with him.

"Hey Bro, come with me."

"Correle compa," said José.

"¿Por qué tanta prisa? Homes!"

"José took me to my grandma's house, which was three blocks away from Edgar's house. One of my uncles who still lived with my grandma was outside sitting down on a rock with his head down, stained with blood all over his white T-shirt.

I thought he had been badly injured in a fight since we usually got into fights with other guys from other barrios that came to ours. My uncle looked like he was crying. He was. I then saw Pablo, another of my uncles who was just sitting on the ground with his back to the wall of the house. He looked exhausted and was also crying. They both had their heads down and I couldn't see their faces very clearly. "No pude hacer nada, It was too late."

Then I looked around and saw my favorite uncle, Jesús, who was laying on the ground, out on the street with blood all over his wounded body. He didn't have on a shirt, and there was blood beneath him on the ground, Jesús had been killed. I didn't know how to respond because I had lost more than just an uncle, he was the best uncle I had. We were very close and very young. It was all due to a stupid fight he had. He had fought with another guy from the barrio next to ours. The other guy used a knife in the middle of the fight and stabbed my uncle several times, causing his death. The other guy ran back to his barrio where we couldn't go after him because his gang would be there to protect him. We didn't want to get the law against the guy, because we knew, we someday would get our revenge.

Three months had gone by and our sorrow still continued deep inside our souls. Rafa was one of my best friends; he was very brave and always willing to help you in anything or against anyone. Rafa was the kind of friend who would back you up when you had to fight another guy from another barrio. I still remember one day when a guy from another barrio had come to ours to beat up some of us. Then

Rafa gave him a really bad beating that he regretted for coming down to our barrio.

The day I most remember was on an Easter Sunday. That morning all the guys from the barrio, including myself, got together to kick it back and then go to our usual weekend soccer game we played every week. We won that day with a goal from Rafa. That afternoon, there was going to be a big dance in celebration of Easter. All kinds of people from the barrios around came to that dance because it was an important event that only occurred once a year. The dance was almost over when the guy who had killed my Uncle Jesus appeared with his whole gang. We didn't worry about it so much because our gang was also there. The guy's name was Justo.

We knew there was going to be a big brawl, barrio against barrio. But Rafa said he would challenge Justo to a clean fist fight to the death. We all agreed to leave the two of them to fight and we gathered in a large circle. Rafa started giving Justo a beating and it looked like Justo had no chance against Rafa who was a great street fighter. Justo then pulled out a knife and cut Rafa on the stomach. Rafa started bleeding, but not much. A guy from our side threw him a knife so Rafa could use it. Rafa rushed against Justo, stabbing him several times on the stomach causing deep penetrations. Justo threw several strikes cutting Rafa on the hands and chest but no real penetrations.

The police sirens could be heard coming from far away. Rafa thought he ought to run since he had hurt Justo badly enough that he was probably going to die pretty soon. So, we all started running, including Rafa. Justo just lay on the ground covered with blood. He was still alive, but he knew there was a lot of possibility that he would die because he had been stabbed many times on the stomach.

Rafa ran because he knew that if the police were to get him, he would probably spend many years in prison. Rafa ran as fast as he could. I was running a couple of feet ahead of him. I turned back to see if Rafa was all right. It was there, that I saw Rafa bleeding. It was a large spurt of blood coming out of his neck. There was a lot of blood and it was coming out of a slice he had received that he didn't even know about.

Rafa fell to the ground. I stopped to pick him up so he could continue running. He couldn't. Rafa had lost a lot of blood and then I knew he was just about to die. Rafa was lying on the ground and I was on my knees next to him. Rafa touched his wound with his left hand.

He only stared at his hand stained with blood. It looked like Rafa was trying to place his hand on top of his wound in order to stop the bleeding. He looked terrified and wasn't able to speak. He was in shock. I tried to help him, so I carried him using my hands and ran as fast as I could run, but it was too late. My house was only one block away and I thought we were going to make it. Rafa was gone, forever, and I had seen him for the last time alive while I carried him with my hands. The saddest moment I still remember, is carrying Rafa, my friend, who was already dead.

Justo somehow managed to survive and served a 15-year prison term for that incident. I'll never forget my uncle Jesús or my friend Rafa.

Why Me?

Luis Solis

"José! There's someone to see you," Maria yelled from the living room to the bedroom.

"Who is it?" He asked.

As he walked towards the living room he knew who it was, the patrón. He had come to tell them to leave, that they couldn't stay there any more. Or maybe he was here to apologize to him.

"Good morning, patrón," José said with great respect. "How are you?"

"Fine thanks," the patrón said with equal respect. "I came here to tell you that I'm sorry for firing you, but I had to, José. We can't have drug addicts working here."

"Yes, patrón, I know," José said weakly.

"That's why I'm going to give you a second chance," the patrón said. "You have to go to a drug rehabilitation clinic for a week, and really work hard at kicking this hindrance, José."

"Yes, patrón! Thank you, thank you," José said thankfully.

"You see José, these guys don't work as good as you do. They do everything half fast. I had to go out there just to make up for your absence. José, you are the best worker I've ever had and the most loyal."

"Thank you patrón, for the compliment. I promise you that I will work harder than ever, after I get out of the clinic."

José did clean up his act and worked harder than ever. The patrón was happy also because he had his friend and best worker back, but also he did not have to work. This pleased him and the workers that had to put up with him for the days he worked. The workers, because they hated that the patrón came down to work with them.

Ten years have passed. I've seen this place change with time. I'm 70, with no family. All I have is this orchard and house. Sure, it's nice, but a family would be, too. José has been the only loyal worker I've had. He's like family. He's become a good foreman; he does the job well and with zeal. I think when I die I might leave all this to him. To my friend and loyal compatriot."

The patrón and José have developed a good friendship after his fight with drugs. The patrón had confided in him, and so did José, so it's no surprise that the patrón did this.

"Patrón! Patrón?" José said, astonished by the news.

"It seems your loyalty to your patrón has rewarded you," the lawyer said.

"Are you sure?" José asked. "This isn't a joke, right?"

"No sir, it's not a joke," the lawyer said. "You're the new owner of this estate. You live in the house, the big one; you own the orchard. Everything. I've got to go. Good luck."

"It's a dream, Maria," José said to his wife, crying with joy.

"It's not José, it's right here in black and white," she said, showing him the will.

"I know, I know," he said. "I'm going to change things, Maria. I'm going to make things better around here."

The workers loved José, their new patrón. The reason was that he made the housing conditions better for all the workers. In addition, because he gave them raises for how hard they worked. They liked working for him, because they knew he had gone through what they were going through, so they respected him.

Young Thoughts

Berenice Garcia

It was a regular hot summer day. The family was out in the fields picking cherries. My sister and I were very excited that day because we would be spending the weekend with my madrina. Our parents were supposed to take us after the day ended.

It was hot and I was tired and hungry. I was picking cherries on the bottom branches of the tree and my mom was on the ladder. My sister was with my dad about one tree ahead of us. After a awhile I moved towards my mom, then suddenly I heard her scream and as I looked up I saw her fall from he tree. I remember my exact third grade words were, "She fell like a bird." Everyone ran to my mom, and my uncle tried pulling at her arm, but the pain was still there. I think he made it worse. We rushed her to the hospital and I remember she laughed as we walked up to Emergency. She said the doctors wouldn't know where to start because it looked like she was bleeding everywhere because of all the cherry stains on her clothes.

My sister and I never got to go with my madrina, that weekend, or any other weekend.

I saw these little bugs in my bucket of cherries one day and froze. I dropped my basket and screamed. I hate bugs. I never again got the nerve to pick cherries. Not even when my dad threatened to punish me if I didn't. What if they got in my ears and I became deaf?

Forget

The couple, my mom and dad, had family on the other side, El Norte. How close of family, that was the question. They helped them and let them live in their house, after all, they were family. Times were hard and work was not too good, but what were they going to do? My mom became pregnant and she could no longer work. That meant there was less money for rent or food. My dad did what he could and they remained in their relative's house.

When winter came it was worse for everyone. There wasn't that much food and everyone became greedy. My mom, still pregnant, would get up early in the morning and cook all the men's lunches. My dad had a big appetite she always put a little extra in for him. After all the other men's wives never got up to cook their lunch.

One day my mom found the refrigerator under chain and lock. My uncle José, whose house it was, had the key. There was no refrigerator and they said my mom ate too much because of her pregnancy and so did my dad, and that they were taking their food. This was the reason given to everyone else.

They owned their own house now and a carne asada was taking place. Friends showed up, even people no one really knew, but they blended in so it was OK. The back yard was full and plates full of food were being served. Through the gate walked Uncle José and his family.

Routine

My name woke me up along with some shoving. It was time to go to work. My eyelids couldn't open, my body was tired and not ready to go. I crawled out of bed, put on the ugliest, oldest jeans I had. The sun was still hiding. My dad was ready and waiting for my sister and me. We hurry and wonder how they could do this every day. Especially for as long as they have been doing it.

Everyone gets in the car and the smell of the calm breeze pours in and the smell of hot coffee is mixed in. My mom talks of how if we hurry and work hard, we'll get home earlier. Earlier I thought, earlier is never early enough. My sister was always more into it than I was.

When we finally got there my mom and dad got out, my sister and me stayed to sleep. After we heard the tractors in the morning we got up and picked cherries. The day finally ended and we were overjoyed, my sister and I. On the way home there was usually always a stop to DQ for ice cream.

We used to have races, my sister and me. We'd run up and down the fields and sometimes we'd slip and fall, but we'd keep going because this was our break from carrying the bucket on our backs. Then there would be singing among all the workers and dirty jokes. We understood some, but not all. Then the grown ups would laugh when we asked what they meant.

Sueños, Dreams Y Recuerdos

Pablo López

My dreams are so wild because they are all mixed in one. One night I started to dream about when I was crossing the border, comencé a soñar que estaba en Los Angeles esperando que mi papá llegara a recogernos. It was fun, because he took us, my family and me, to Disneyland. Well, we didn't come in, because we only passed by. We were scared of the migra because we didn't want them to take us back to México.

The next day I woke up and I was scared. I don't know why, that the only thing I know is that when I was dreaming, I was running away from something. I don't know what it was, but I was running away from it.

I remember one time when my grandfather was telling me a story about the Huicholes, he told me that one day when he was a young man, he used to walk on the sierra where he lived. He was walking one morning and he heard something in a barranca and went to see what was going on. He had never heard anything like that before around there, and he went to see. When he got close he saw an animal, a kind of animal he had never seen before. It was a big snake with two heads, and he was scared when he saw the big snake. He ran faster, as fast as he could, and when he got home, he told this to his father, what he had seen in the barranca.

His father said, "¿Hijo cómo va a ser una víbora con dos cabezas y que mida 5 metros de largo? ¿estás seguro que no andas borracho como otros días?" And my grandfather said, "¿Cómo crees apá? hoy no ando tomado, ni siquiera me he arrimado a la cantina hoy." And his father said, "Está bien. Vamos a ver si es cierto que hay una víbora en la barranca, pero no más que no sea verdad ya verás lo que voy a hacerte, para que no andes diciendo mentiras."

They went to the barranca to see if the big snake was there or not, and when they got there, my great grandfather said, "Hay caramba, creo que esta vez está diciendo la verdad," and my grandfather said, "Y eso que todavía no le ve la cabeza, porque se va a asustar cuando la mire, porque está fea de a de veras parece el demonio."

And he and his father walked to the snake, and his father was scared, but my grandfather told him that it was OK because the snake was sleeping and they could get closer to see if it was alive or if it was dead.

When they got closer they saw that the snake was opening an eye to see if there was something around to eat, because the snake tried to eat my grandfather, but he could go away from the snake, and they ran to the town to get the rifle to kill the big snake. When they got back to the town, other men were coming with them, but they couldn't kill the snake with the rifles because the balas wouldn't penetrate the snake's skin. So the only thing they did was that they started to pray and pray until a big star came down from the sky and killed the big snake. Everybody was saying that it was the evil one who was coming out from the wild. That's what my grandfather told me when I was ten years old, and he said that this was true.

VI. A Final Story

Eva Siddhartha Valdivia

For the first time in many years I felt that I no longer wanted to pretend.

Eva Siddhartha Valdivia

Eva Siddhartha Valdivia

Eva Siddhartha Valdivia

When I won the HAPP scholarship, it was a hard-earned accomplishment. I was very proud of myself. During my introduction at the banquet I started to approach the stage with my mother. Once I was there I saw lots of eyes looking at me and only me looking back. I was standing there while someone described what I had done to be worthy of the scholarship awarded. That night they put the medallion around my neck, shook my hand, and congratulated my mother and myself. Tears came down my eyes. I was happy but something didn't feel right. I asked myself, "Oh god now what?.."

I was really nervous. In a way, I felt I was cheating or using the system because I didn't have papers, yet they were giving me a scholarship. I could not stop thinking what they might do if they knew they were giving a scholarship " una Ilegal". I had to calm myself. I couldn't let the people who were standing by me know what I was feeling or get too emotionally carried away or they might ask. I then thought, No, I am here for a reason! Because I worked hard, This is happening. After all, I do possess the talents for which they are recognizing me, so it is O.K. I deserve it. I should not feel guilty.

With that in mind, my mother and I were stepping down the stage. I looked at her eyes and face. She seemed pleased for the first time ever. We were holding hands walking to our destination. We had to go through tables and aisles to get to our table on the other side of the room. Here I was passing through and getting compliments from people and my mother holding my hand tighter and tighter. People were looking approvingly at us.

Soon they were going to wrap up the program. I stared at my mother's eyes and she stared back but not for long. A minute after they invited people to stay for the dance. I told myself, "Now here's some relief." I focused on the dance. Dancing is my thing: my language, my other place of pleasure and peace. The world where I may get as wild as I want. The world where no one can stop me. The only world where I have total control. The world where I don't have to pretend and I can be myself. For the first time in many years I no longer wanted to pretend.

When my mother heard about the invitation for the dance she wanted to go home. Dancing wasn't something she was pleased about. Her religious beliefs about dancing were very strict. She had a strong belief that dancing only made it more possible to have sexual encounters. That being the case I walked them to the door and said good-night.

Right when they left I went to speak with my dear friend and her husband. I consider them both like my mother and father. That night I had the privilege to have them accompany me. They are always so busy that it was a real happiness for me to have their presence there with me that night. I told them I wanted to stay for the dance. Maud told me it was O.K., that she would take Thalia home with her.

With that being the case I stayed for the dance. I saw some acquaintances there. I danced all night long. I was in my own little world where I felt comfortable and at peace.

I picked up some different energy and my mood quickly changed. I felt it very clearly, a voice that told me not to worry that everything would be O.K. It reminded me of the feelings I experienced when a loved one died. Suddenly I saw him lying in bed with his eyes closed like that day he died. I didn't know exactly what to do, I was stunned, I didn't know what to think of it. I was such a weird feeling I didn't understand it, then.

I didn't know whether to stay there or leave. I knew it was a very special night for me. I was supposed to have fun and be happy. I was just stunned because I was having these flashbacks and I didn't understand why.

Soon the music changed and I started to get more into the dancing energy. I saw lots of friends that I went to school with when I was in middle school. It was interesting how we had all taken different routes going towards high school and I had not seen many in so many years and they were there that night. I danced with different friends all night long. Most I knew.

Juan caught my attention. He was one of my classmates when I first came to the States and enrolled in school, and I have known him ever since. He has always treated me with respect. Juan's family was very poor, and he was always hustling to make an honest dollar. I think most wanted to be more like him, but their false pride or laziness kept them from selling food or other items door to door. Juan did what he had to in order to survive.

Juan had his own individual look, and many used to make fun of him because he looked "different." These hateful remarks always hit him hard. Juan did what he had to do to survive. He became a fighter, and a good one. I knew Juan was not a saint, but I admired him for being himself, always striving to assist his family, and for fighting back. It was interesting how we each had developed our own way of fighting back to survive. So different and yet here we were dancing together.

When we were dancing he told me lots of things. Some of the words that I remember the most were as follows. "Remember that you are the kind of person we, 'los humildes', and many other people admire and look up to as trailblazers. 'Sigue adelante y vence las barreras. Y si en algo te sirvo tú no más dices pa' qué soy bueno'. I hope you go as far as you want to. Achieve what you want. I'm sure that whatever it is you will do or want to be, you will be very good at it. And don't worry, everything will be O.K. only if you keep trying.

That was an unusual experience for me. I knew Juan but I didn't. I'm a very private person. I didn't know him well enough to share anything so private or out of the ordinary. I didn't really know how to take this. I didn't feel he was coming on to me. I felt we had more respect than that. I realized then, he was truly being sincere. He was very positive like never before. That night was sure full of memories and surprises. For the first time in nine years it felt good to hear those words from a classmate.

It was peculiar to me that out of all the people and friends I knew he was the one to tell me these things. But I just smiled. Soon the dance was over and everyone was getting ready to go home. I smiled big time and waived to Juan, "Good-bye." He and his friends waived back. That was the last time I saw Juan.

Next morning an article in the newspaper came out and said that he drowned trying to save some ducks that were tangled with weeds and stuff in the lake at Sportsman's Park. He was working there at the time, cleaning and cutting the grass. Apparently his work partner went in to try to save him but he could not see underwater, it was really dirty. He himself was having trouble.

Sometimes it is so hard for me to understand why some people die and others are allowed to stay. I often feel that life is unfair, and people don't make sense. I am happy that if Juan had to die, that I was the last person he danced with. I strongly feel that this was a privilege, a gift, a memory I should hold in my heart and not let it go. Looking back now, I see it was both a premonition of my life taking an unexpected turn and a reassurance that everything would be O.K.

Sunday came. I got ready to leave. I was going to Seattle for my daughter's birthday celebration. I went to put gas in my car. All of my life has been strange and out of the ordinary. This would be one of those days. I checked the oil, water, and air in the tires. I hit the road. As I was getting close to Ellensburg my stereo started going crazy on me. It kept going through all of the stations really fast and no matter what button I pushed it would not stop. It was a weird thing. I felt this energy coming at me…la vida.

I turned my car on, ready to leave. Then I just did it. I opened the door and went after that piece of paper. It looked like those inside the Chinese fortune cookies. It said, "Smile someone loves you" " Follow your dreams". As soon as I read that I just knew. I just knew that if it wasn't Juan it had to be someone who really did care, like my father or my brother or somebody. And the spirit of that somebody was inside my car. Who ever it was it was in my car. I cried, maybe it was silly but not for me. I felt that presence and I just really believe it was somebody trying to get me a message. Un mensaje que de veras me hizo fortalecerme más como mujer y como persona.

A message that really strengthened me more as a woman and as a person.

Desde ese día todo cambió para mi. I felt that, what I was going through was not in vain. And I also believe I had to do what I had to do. I learned I had to leave many things behind including people I love and many family traditions. I also accepted I could no longer keep everybody happy and I no longer wanted to either. I wanted my life back, the one I let the world take away from me.

I have always been so worried about what people say and think ever since I came here. Even though I had made really hard decisions in the past, I wasn't really sure if that was what I needed to do or wanted to have done. But ever since that moment I felt stronger. I suddenly felt this energy coming at me making me feel like I could do anything or become anything I wanted, if I was determined. It was such a good feeling. En ese momento me sentí la mujer más envidiada y privilegiada del mundo que quería gritar y compartir lo hermoso que es la vida."

I got to Seattle. I did what I had to do to have all the stuff ready for the party that day. I was anxious for the party to be over. I was really tired. I really didn't feel like celebrating anything. Especially after all I had been through days before. Everything went well. Thalia was really happy and so was every one else. But that happiness didn't last for long.

Michael took Thalia from me while I was sleeping. Apparently he wanted to take her away from me to show me that he was a man I needed to watch out for. He went to Santa Rosa, California to see Thalia's godparents.

I purchased a ticket to Santa Rosa, California. I left as soon as possible. I didn't take anything other than what I had on and all of the credit cards. When I got to Santa Rosa I went to my "comadre's" house. Apparently I had just missed Michael. He was there with my daughter. He wanted to leave her there with my "comadre", but she refused because she didn't agree with what he was doing.

She told me he was headed for México. He wanted to take Thalia to meet his grandmother. Michael told her that he only wanted me to see what he can do and show me "que el era un hombre de cuidado". She told me that he loved me very much, but that she thought he was very obsessed.

I almost panicked. I knew I couldn't easily go to México because I had no way to come back safely. She told me he was headed to LA to his uncle's house. He was going to see a friend about giving him a certified letter giving him my permission to take my daughter with him.

All I knew at that moment was that I needed to get to L.A. as soon as possible. I asked my compadre if he would please take me. He saw me so desperate that he felt he had no choice. We took off immediately.

He only dropped me off. He had a restaurant business, so he had to go back as soon as possible. He told me he wished he could stay with me, but that he couldn't. He wished me luck. When I went inside his uncle's house there were a lot of men there. His wife wasn't home. They all seemed pretty rude and Machistas. I asked if they knew where Michael was. They told me he had gone to the Safeway store. They told me it was about four blocks away from the house.

I wasn't really thinking at the time. All I wanted was to see my daughter and Michael face to face. I went walking to the store. His uncle didn't even offer any help. I don't think he cared anyway. I took off for the store. Downtown there was a lot of business and people walking, selling stuff. Near a store I saw a lot of commotion. I saw a van and people with handcuffs. The police or whoever they were, were taking people inside the van.

I then realized it was Immigration. The van sign said so. I got scared, so I stopped and went into another store nearby. I was waiting for the officials to leave. Suddenly a lot of people from that store started to run. They were screaming "La Migra. La migra está por aquí vamonos." I saw all these people running and screaming "la migra." I started running too, going back the way I came. I was running. I then slowed down. I walked normal, I didn't want to seem suspicious.

At that moment I wasn't even thinking about my daughter or Michael. I just wanted to get to his uncle's house.

A block before I got to the house a van pulled over by my side. They stopped right beside me, but I kept walking. It seemed that all of my blood went from my head totally to the ground. They got out and they told me, "Excuse me, Miss, did you get out of the store right back there?" I turned around and I just knew who they were. I told myself, well I won't run, because if I do they'll catch me anyway. I asked "Who are you, may I ask?" One who seemed in charge reach into his pocket and showed me a badge. He said, "L.A Immigration." I told them, "Oh in that case. Yes, I just went to the store and I just got out of there." He said, "Could you show me some identification please?" I said sure. I was looking for my driver's license. I was so nervous and I think they noticed it. I was shaking like I never have before in my life. I couldn't even get my driver's license.

Next they asked me if I was a US citizen. I told them no. He then said, "Could we see your documentation please?" I told them I didn't have them with me, that I had left them home. I told them I was only there for a few days. I told them I was from Washington State. He said that everyone knows better than to travel with out papers and especially in California where there is a rule that people who are not citizens carry their legal papers with them at all times like your driver's license. I told them I didn't really think about it, that at the time of my departure I was in a hurry. It was a family emergency situation.

I was so nervous and so shaky I couldn't think clearly. I didn't even know what I was saying. I was trying so hard not to look suspicious, but I don't think it worked. They asked me why I had to leave in such a hurry. I didn't know what to tell them. I didn't know whether to tell them the truth, which they probably won't believe or make something up. I just felt I couldn't lie. I was so nervous about lying. I felt I wouldn't be able to go through with it. So I told them the truth. I was there because I had come to get my daughter because my husband had taken her with out my knowing, and I was not very happy. I wanted to see them both.

He told me, "I'm sorry ma'am." I'm sure everything will be all right. You have your driver's license so that's a plus. I'm sure you have your papers because without them you can't get a driver's license, but while we clear that up you have to come with us. I asked "Why?" "Well that's part of the process," he said. "You have nothing to worry about if everything is in order."

The problem was that everything was not in order. I felt like crying but I knew I couldn't. I had to hold it. That was really hard. I didn't want to say anything. I knew I was not thinking straight. I decided to stay quiet so that I would not say something that could make things worse. The guys were nice. They only told me to get inside the van. They told me that because I was nice they were not going to handcuff me.

I asked them if it would be O.K. to make a phone call. I told them I needed to tell my family where I was. They told me not to worry that they will take care of it as soon as we got to the immigration office.

We got to the immigration office. They put me in an office that was pretty much made up of windows. I could see lots of people doing their job and stuff. Finally the two men that had picked me up came back. They had lots of paper work. They asked for my driver's license. They copied everything in it. Then they started to ask the questions. Personal questions. I was feeling very uncomfortable.

Finally. I told them I wanted to make a phone call. They let me, but stayed right there listening. I called Michael's uncle and told him that Immigration had me and I needed him to tell Michael so that he could maybe bring me all of the documentation and they might let me go. He was very stunned I think. All he would do was listen. He knew I had no papers whatsoever. He told me not to worry that they would take care of everything for me so that I would be all right. Then they told me that was all the time they had.

I didn't know exactly what they were doing. Everything to me seemed very mysterious, as if they were hiding something. I felt that for some reason all the questioning and the special attention was not part of the process when they arrest someone for being illegal.

After I hung up they left me all alone. It took a while before they came back. I could see them getting on the phone, going back and forth talking with each other. When they came back they asked more questions. They asked me for my social security number and when I got my green card. I told them I didn't know my social security number by memory, and that I got my green card about eight years ago.

I knew that was the biggest lie ever, but they didn't know that. I felt it was my best chance. I was very sad. At that moment I couldn't think. I didn't really want to. Before I had everything in my mind. I was thinking about where I was supposed to be at. School. I knew I had to be in school. I knew I needed my daughter with me and to know that she was all right. I needed to talk with her father. I really had a lot of things to think about.

I asked God for strength. I told him I will deal with whatever was to happen but I asked him to please take care of my family. I was in a corner with no exit. I felt trapped and the worse part was that I couldn't do anything about it. Someone else had control of my life.

Soon they came back again and told me that they couldn't find anything on me. That being the case, they were going to have to keep me until they found something on me or until they could clear stuff up. I knew I didn't want to be there and that it wasn't my choice so I let them do whatever they needed to do.

They took my clothes away and everything I had. They gave me some blue pants and a blue long sleeve shirt with some sleepers. I changed and they took me to a cell. I was in a cell for a day all by myself. Afterwards they changed me to a big room full of women. There were lots of beds. I felt so uncomfortable and sad.

Apparently all the women there were illegal. Some of them were caught trying to pass with a "coyote". Others working. Some already knew the routine because they had been there several times. But they told me, "They are not going to stop me."

I am a shy and really private person. No acostumbro to converse with someone if I haven't been properly introduced. I feel I'm being an intruder when I approach somebody without a purpose. But nobody there felt like that. As soon as they showed me my bed, lots of women came to talk to me, to learn what had happened and to share their experience.

Most of them did not speak English. Almost all of them seemed very poor and illiterate. They were all so sad. I guess they felt that's the way it had to be. If it meant they had to go through that I bet almost everyone would do it, over and over until they crossed to the other side. To "El Norte".

I was very uncomfortable there. I felt like I didn't fit in. It was one of the saddest days of my life. Once I was there I started to think all of those things I was trying to avoid thinking at the beginning. I was going through them one by one in my head and most of them just killed me. I knew I wasn't supposed to be there. I felt that I belonged somewhere else.

Here I was in a cell with a whole bunch of women and some children. A cell where they told me what to do and when to do it. A cell where I had no liberty. Where someone else had control of what I did. A cell where I no longer was myself, an "abrecaminos for many."

Yes! There I was paying a price for being who I am and becoming what I dream. Siddhartha Eva Valdivia was locked up after winning a two thousand dollar scholarship that will pay her college expenses. A scholarship that I worked very hard for and that would have given me an opportunity to get others, if I had my papers.

It was quite a dramatic change, going in one moment from being a total winner to a total loser, with the exception that I knew I was still a winner on the inside. The circumstances on the outside had become more difficult, but that didn't change me—who I am or my capabilities. I was still determined to achieve my goals.

Next morning as we went through the routine and the officials treated us like we were nothing, they pulled me out and took me to an office. There I was questioned again. Pretty much the same things. I was told not to worry about my daughter and husband, they were all right. Michael wanted to see me, but that would not be allowed. What was surprising was that one of the officers asked me, "So, which college are you planning to go to?"

I was stunned. I hesitated to answer but I was looking at him straight in the eyes. All I said was, "The University of Washington in Seattle." "And your major?" I said, "Teaching and Psychology." He told me, "Well, that's interesting. Good luck."

I didn't know what to say. But the way he was talking to me, it seemed that I was free to go. I didn't know what to say, so I stayed quiet. I was waiting for more questions, but all they were doing was going through paper work and looking at me. Then they told me "Well, that is all for today. Thank you! Sgt. Corrales will accompany you back to your cell."

At least I was relieved to know that my daughter and Michael were found and he knew where I was. Talking to the officer and answering those questions confused me. But now I was tranquil, and more relieved.

When I got back some of the women asked me what they had wanted. All I told them was that the officials had started to question me again. One of the women there said that all they do all the time is question and question the women. Sometimes they even slap them because none are willing to say the name of the "coyote" that helped them pass through or give them any information.

That place smelled so bad! The walls were so dirty. It seemed like the air was poisoned because it was not fresh. I felt I couldn't even breathe right. The sheets smelled like old clothes. The clothes we were wearing smelled pretty bad too. The only thing that was yours in there was your underwear. You couldn't even wear your brassiere. Everything was just so wrong.

I decided that in order to be more at peace I would sleep and go to that "other" world. I didn't want to hear anybody. All I wanted to do was rest. So I went to sleep. I don't know how long. They woke me up so that we could go eat, but I didn't feel like eating. The food there grossed me out. It was nasty. So I didn't eat. I gave my food away.

When we went back to the big room, everyone went to their own beds. I didn't feel like sleeping since I had slept almost all afternoon. Ten minutes later they turned the lights off. It was very dark. You couldn't see anything. Soon I got used to the darkness so I could see a little, like shadows. I started thinking, *How will it be if I have to go back to México?*

I remembered when I was a little girl. Mi infancia. My infancy. How different it was from the life over here. I remembered how I didn't even want to come over here to begin with. I was really happy as a little girl. I didn't know how happy I was down there, until all of that was taken away from me.

Soon my eyes got tired. Finally I went to sleep. I woke up next morning and almost everyone was awake. We all got in line to go wash ourselves. The showers were pretty nasty and I felt kind of uncomfortable because there were no curtains, no nothing! There were only showers. Everyone had to be there washing up, completely nude and without privacy. All we got was a tiny little towel to dry. We didn't even get to wash our underwear. You had to put the same dirty clothes back on.

Afterwards, we got to eat breakfast. By that time I was so hungry I ate the food even though I didn't like it. Then we went back to the room. A couple of police officers came, and took about ten women that were there. According to the women, the officers were taking them because they were getting them ready to leave to México. The bus was going to take them to the border.

At that moment I felt really sad for them and for myself. I asked them how come they only took them and not all of us. They said that they usually keep you there for three days. Apparently they do a lot of investigation and a lot of paper work. Not all the women there are caught the same day so that's how come some leave early others don't.

In my mind I was getting ready to accept the fact I was going back without being ready. I was already thinking what I would be doing once they drop me in the border. It was such a terrible feeling—tears came out each time I would think about it.

Later some women gathered and they started praying. They started praying for themselves and for the ones that were gone already. I felt I couldn't do anything else other than to share my pain and faith with them. So I went beside them. I started to pray, too. I wasn't praying out loud. I was quiet. After we all finished praying, I felt more at peace. I was ready to go lay down in that bed. Lots of tears came down when I was praying. I was exhausted by the time it was over.

A few hours later they came to get me. I didn't ask anything. I just went where they took me. They took me to the same room that had all those windows when I first arrived. I was sitting there with the officer while another officer came in and had a bag with him. All of my stuff was inside. He told me, "Here's your stuff, Mrs. Rodriguez. You can have it to change. Please do so now!" They took me to a restroom, where I changed and combed my hair.

When I got out, an officer was waiting for me. He took me back to the room with the windows. He told me to go in and that he would be back in a little bit. I waited there for a while and then they came in. He told me to please sign those papers. I was about to start reading them when he said, "It only states you are free to go. That's for us to keep records and stuff. Your husband is waiting for you outside." I looked up and sure enough Michael was waiting there for me. He wasn't looking at the room.

I could see out, but he couldn't see in. I don't think he knew where I was. Tears came down my eyes. I read the piece of paper quickly and it was true. The officer was saying the truth. I signed and got up. They told me, "Sorry for all of the trouble."

I didn't really know what was going on. I didn't understand anything. It didn't make any sense that they were letting me go, someone who didn't have any papers. I didn't ask questions. All I knew was that they were letting me go and that's what I wanted. I got my purse and went outside. As soon as I opened the door, I saw Michael.

He came towards me and I went towards him. I hugged him. He told me, "I'm sorry, Eva, I'm sorry!" I told him I wanted to get out of there. We both walked outside and it was true, I was free. Tears came down for a long time. I could not believe what was happening. Michael asked about how I was treated in there. I asked him how come they let me go? He told me he wasn't ready to talk about it. I myself wasn't ready to talk about it either, and I told him so.

We went to his uncle's house. As soon as I walked in, I saw my daughter sitting on the couch. She saw me and ran towards me. I waited for her. I hugged her and gave her a big kiss. I held her tight for a few minutes. I was so happy to see her. I was happy to be back with my baby.

So many things had happened that I wasn't really sure what I was to do. A lot of my energy was taken. I felt like I wanted to rest and head home as soon as possible. When we got to the house Michael's uncle could not believe I was back. He did not question me. I think Michael told them not to.

Even though I was really mad at Michael for what he had done my heart did not have any room for resentment. I was not ready to confront him. All I wanted was for my daughter and him to be by my side.

Two days later we went home to Seattle. His family had already known what had happened to me. They couldn't believe I was there. They thought I was somewhere in México. I didn't really want to talk about it. I think they got the hint. Michael's mother calls it a miracle and so does everyone else. His father does not believe it. He thinks we were making that up. He says, "There's no way that if Immigration got me they let me go." He says, "That's a whole bunch of bull shit."

But I know it is true because it happened to me. I, too, like Michael's mom call it a miracle that changed my life forever. A miracle that I'm so thankful for and that I give God thanks for opening my eyes and giving me another chance. I would never wish for someone to go through that. But if it had to be the way it was for me, then welcome to the world.

My family back home did not know a word about what was going on. Still to this day they know nothing. I didn't want them to resent Michael. They don't really like him, and I just didn't need any more tension. I felt it was a lesson for me, a message that I should pay attention to and deal with alone. I really wasn't ready to share that experience with them or anybody else. I wanted to keep it for me and only for me.

Time passed before I called Maud and told her I was all right. I don't even remember what I told her. I knew she was going to be sad and confused about my behavior, but I just couldn't tell her. I knew I was supposed to be in school finishing up, but I also knew I couldn't. I had arrangements to finish that summer but everything changed for me. I was not really focused anymore. I was very confused.

So I decided to stay down in Seattle. School was out already. I knew I was supposed to be in summer school, but I was not ready to go. Some part of me wanted to, but the other, and the strongest, didn't want to. I was just not ready. I needed some time. I needed time to think things through, and analyze what had happened and see where I wanted to go and do.

I decided not to think about what I was suppose to be doing. It was summer and I had the opportunity to relax, so I did.

I had so many decisions to make, important decisions, that I didn't know anymore if what I was doing was right for me or the best thing to do. As time passed I realized I was getting overwhelmed. It was just driving me crazy. I decided not to think about it anymore. I figured that if I kept going on like that, I wasn't going to get to be old. So I put it off until school started. I decided that I was going to go to school next year. I decided I wanted to get my high school diploma. That's what I have always wanted, and I wasn't going to settle for less.

For five years I let somebody else run my life. That wasn't going to be the case here anymore. Many people had disappointed me. Some discouraged me from pursuing my dreams. I was no longer going to allow that. Even the school system was a disappointment. It was sad for me to see and hear how so many were encouraged to just settle for less and go the easy route. Not me! Fuck them I said.

I started school in September. I didn't want a full schedule. I knew I was faced with so many responsibilities and decisions. I didn't want to get more frustrated. School has always been an important part of my life. Soy una persona detallista. When it comes to school work I'm a very picky person. I either do it all or I don't do it at all! That's why I didn't want a full load. I had decided to get my diploma. I was willing to do whatever was necessary. I also knew my heart wasn't there, I wasn't all there.

I needed to figure out many things and accept them. I realized that if I wanted to have a good life I couldn't keep running and let things get fixed by themselves or pretend they were O.K. I needed to take care of them. So I knew something had to be done. And I knew I had to change how I was doing things so I could progress.

With all of those thoughts in my mind I was going to school. I continued going and I knew I wanted to be there, but in a way I didn't feel motivated. I had to do many things I didn't want to. I wasn't happy. I have a lot of pride. That's my nature. Even though life had taught me to control it and modify it is still there in some part of me.

I knew I wanted to do this. I wanted to get this over with, yet I wasn't willing to add frustration to my life. I really didn't want to face so many things. In a way I still kept running. I knew what I had to do, but I wouldn't do it. I was fine that way so I didn't do anything really.

But soon time kept going. Many things I could stop but time certainly wasn't one of them. Time kept going and I kept staying behind. I wasn't ahead of it anymore. I was angry and sad. I was furious. I had many chances to get this over with and I didn't.

Then I started thinking. One day I was all alone. Really it was how it always was. I just never really thought about it that hard. I remembered that time in jail and I remembered how fortunate and lucky I am. I remember the prayers at the jail and what one woman said, "We are not asking for an easy life, only to be stronger, Lord" What she said stayed in my mind. I had heard it before, but never with so much meaning. That's how I felt about life too. I remembered all of that and what I had gone through in these last years.

I was mad. Very angry at myself. Finally I decided to prioritize things. I knew I had many things and decisions to make, but I also knew that it would be very foolish to try to do them all at once. I determined that if I wanted to go further and embrace my life I was the only one with that power. Nobody else can do that. I know for a fact that I would not have been able to get by with out the help of the people who care about me, but they could only do so much. I was angry enough to start doing what I should have a long time ago.

I had never seen myself in that attitude before. Suddenly I became so powerful. My anger was a good kind of anger. I took my time doing things. I got busy! I believed in myself again. I felt once again that staying true to myself and sticking to what I believe— only then things will work out. It doesn't matter if anybody else believes in me. It doesn't matter whether it was right or not, it just was what I believe. Being faithful to that was the real challenge, because I knew the emptiness and unhappiness when I wasn't.

Now I'm discovering new things about myself and the people around me. Uncovering things from the past. Things that were taken from me and that belong to me. Starting to say what needs to be said. And doing many things I didn't want to before. But that is all good. Real good as a matter of fact! I feel at peace and with a road ahead of me. This feeling is so great that I can't even describe it. I wish everyone in the world will get the chance to feel this way. Because it's great! Because it's the best! Because it's the power!

I live in two worlds. They are so different, so unique. When I came to the States back in '89 I thought people over here had everything all backwards. I remember when I first arrived it started to snow. That was the first time in my life I had ever seen it. I remember I told my mother that the world was going to end because white stuff was coming from the sky. She started laughing. She told me that was called snow, and that it snows during the winter in the states and it gets really cold.

Life was not the same. While I was in school I met a very special person in my life. She and her family have become part of my family. I consider her and her husband like my father and mother. She is someone who I really admire and look forward to talk to.

Our relationship started many years back when I first came to the United States. Maud had a program after school where she taught dance, art, music, and singing. I didn't speak English whatsoever but that didn't keep me from being curious. I jointed "Los Bailadores Del Sol" a Mexican folklore group that occupied the facility where Maud had her program. They both shared the same facility. When Maud was getting ready to leave we would come in. Sometimes I would come a little early and would see her teaching tap dancing to the kids. All I could do was stare. I thought it was so neat how they were able to make those noises with their feet.

Pretty soon Maud noticed I liked it. She invited me to dance. I didn't really know what she was saying but I could see her hand inviting me to go dance with her. I accepted and I tried it. I liked it very much. All I would do is copy what she was doing and little by little I learned English. Soon that's how I learned to understand her. I kept coming back. I was pretty consistent so we started to know more about each other.

I used to look forward to go dance with her. I didn't know anybody and I felt comfortable with her. That is why going with Maud was my only way of relief. But I do not know what happened really, I didn't.

Now I'm getting to know myself closer. Each time it gets better. I'm on a journey that doesn't really have a path. I'm learning everyday and I listen. I'm a seeker. I plan to continue beyond my high school education. I don't know if it would really help me become more intellectual or totally the contrary. I know I could get a better job. Maybe that's the reason that I want to pursue it. For my financial stability and to provide the best for my daughter.

I want to go back to my home country if not to live just to visit. I also want to find and see if the man who brought me into this world is still alive. I would very much like to meet him and tell him I had the opportunity to name myself unlike many, many people. See what this guy is about. Most likely changes will be occurring for me. I like that. I would also like to travel around the world. Go to Spain and take flamenco classes in Seville. Learn many things from people and their cultures and offer back what made me Siddhartha Eva Valdivia.

VII. About the Authors & Vocabulario

I have four sisters and three brothers, and one of my brothers is my twin.

Leticia

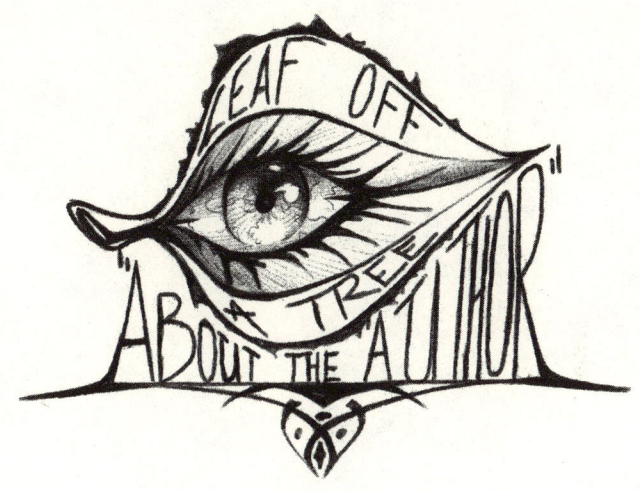

Vocabulario / Vocabulary

Con Mis Mãnos Llenas

abrecaminos: This is an example. We are all examples. We never stop working or searching. We open paths that help others to be successful. You can be the abrecaminos in your family, just by helping others. My mother is an abrecaminos. A person with hope to win. Siempre hay un lugar donde puedas encontrar un abrecaminos. There's always a place where we can find an abrecaminos, too. You have to have the desire to be an example for other people. This person makes a path where there is no path, and it is easy for more people to go through. Rigoberta Menchú is an abrecaminos. You can be one, too. This is who we are. We make a way. Be an abrecaminos and get to work. A chain breaker. For me, Gloria Anzaldúa is an abrecaminos.

alma: Soul. The Aztecs have two words for soul. *Tonal*, or *alma*; and *nagual*, or other self, like a plant or animal spirit. Our souls guide us in our lives.

abuelito/a: Grandfather. An abuelo is considered the head of the family in our culture We honor our grandparents by showing respect to their lives. Apá grande.

agua: Water. The water gives us the future.

amargo: Bitter. I have a bitter heart. Esto nos enseña que no todo es fácil en la vida y hay qué seguir luchando para alcanzar el propio potencial.

amante: Lover. In some parts to be lovers is still considered very bad because of the high morals of our families.

amar: To love. We need to learn to love ourselves.

amor: Love. I want to know the meaning of love.

baboso/a: He will talk stuff that will make him seem stupid. This is someone who hasn't yet understood their purpose in life. Una persona que sale con puras babosadas. He wants to act childish and not understand.

barreras: Barriers. Another word for chains. An abrecaminos is someone who breaks the barreras. This is for life or death. Crossing land. If you make it, it is where you could find life, but sometimes sorrow.

bromas: A way to laugh, show how you care, seeing people laughing and being happy. Persona humorosa. Jokes.

cadenas: Chains. *Romper cadenas* means to break chains.

calor: Heat, glow. Her heat lives within me.

calle: Street. A street is no dream.

canela: Sabor excelente ¡Oye, ese!/¿Te gusta el agua?/¿A qué sabe?/El agua es buena para todos/Pero, es como la leche/Sabe mejor con sabores/Así como en un aula mixta/de diferentes chicos/O una ensalada mixta/en vez de sólo una cosa/Hay muchas cosas que saben bien/ en combinación con otras/¡Pero, no hay nada que sepa/mejor que la canela, ese!/Sé orgulloso de quién eres/No rechases tu cultura/tu ser/tu familia/ ni el mundo completo/Sé orgullos o de quién eres/De tu piel canela/ Torito

camino: Road, course. Senda. No one knows when the road ends. The way we go. Path.

canción: Song. This song reminds me of you.

casa: House. I spent my infancy in that house of white walls.

compa: The best friend of a guy. Or a compadre of a guy or a woman. Your compa is the best farmer in the valley. To be or not to be. Friend. Partner.

conocer: To know. It is laborious to know the woman of the illusion.

coyote: He is someone that helps you cross the border from México to the US. El coyote es muy astuto y sabe lo que esta haciendo. Persona que pega por detras. Malero. He can be good or he can be bad. There are coyotes in the desert. El coyote es mi nagual.

corazón: Heart. My heart died when she vanished.

Chilango/a: A person from the Capital, from Mexico City. Negative.

Pejorative.

curandera/o: Someone who heals pain the old way. My grandma was a curandera. The curandera knows the earth, the culture, the yerbas. She has a better understanding of life. Healer of body and of heart. She knows more medicine than any doctor. La curandera vendrá a curar el hechiso que tengo por dentro. Every traditional mother is a curandera.

destino: destiny. I have to follow my destiny until the end. Mi destino es cuidar a mi familia.

dinero: Money. Money is not everything in life. Lana. Jando, Feria. Plata.

dicho: Es un refran que se refiere o habla de cosas, personas o animales y nos enseña algo. *Every time an old person dies, a library burns*. Like that. De tal palo tal astilla.

dolor: Pain, grief. Grief is what describes me.

en: In, at, on. I will die in battle for her.

enojado: Angry. Anger, enojo, exists like motivation. Petroleo. Like poison inside a snake.

esperanza: Hope. Hope is the last thing in a human being.

espina: Thorn. You left a thorn inside of me.

estrella: star. You are like a star, so high to reach.

feliz: happy, content (felicidad) happiness. Everyone has to find the happiness in the life cycle.

flor: Flower. The flower of my garden.

florecer: To blossom. My rose would never blossom. Flor de amor and confusion. And flower of long distant relationship.

gorditas de harina. A very delicious snack that is really like a cookie. It is a mixture of oil, water, sugar, and flour. After mixing all this, I would cook them on a griddle.

frontera: The border. It's not only a line that separates, but inside the line it's another world. Son barreras que se ponen en nuestros caminos and sometimes it is hard to take them out of our paths. The borders are hard for immigrants to cross. La frontera está en Nogales y Texas.

fresa: Strawberry. Metaphor for snob.

ganas: The strength that comes deep from our souls that gives us the impulse to go on, and fight through struggles that come, to be someone in life, and abrecaminos we will become. Es la voluntad, la esperanza que uno tiene en la vida. This is the power to put something, sometimes ourselves, into other worlds.

Green Card: A compact wall that is built by the fear of the insecure. And blindness. A piece of paper por el cual mucho gente ha muerto. Lots of people have died because they didn't have the Green Card. Permiso para trabajar.

Guadalupana: Es tener sangre India pura y tener orgullo de lo que vale cada ser humano. Para mi es tener alma y corazón. It means life to me. A woman gives birth, and, in a way, she gave birth to God. We are all the sons and daughters of La Virgin.

hijos: Children. The children are the gift of God.

humilde: Humble. My mother is a humble woman.

imagenes de mujeres: There's more to us than Malinche or Guadalupe, virgen o mala mujer. A dentro de la Malinche hay muchos imagenes: abrecamino, amante, politíco, madre, bilingüe—multi-lingüe, multicultural. There is Sor Juana, Rosario Castellanos, Cisneros, Anzaldúa, our mothers, Laura Esquivel. Somos muchas.

ingenio de azucar: A place where sugar is processed from *caña* to sugar.

ilusión: Illusion. My illusion is you. Like fire from heaven.

I.N.S.: Another wall for us. Dream stoppers. Otra barrera.

jornada: Journey. We *say jornada sagrada*, meaning *sacred journey*. It's how we live our lives and how we study, too. Another word is *peregrinaje*, or pilgrimage.

lana: Metaphor Mexicans use for money. See *dinero*. Wool in the dictionary.

lágrima: Tear. This tear is for her. Hay lágrimas de tristeza y lágrimas de alegría.

luna: Moon. The moon understands my mind.

machismo: A macho is a man who thinks he can do everything, but the woman can't. Why do men think that. They are *machistas*. What is the word for machista in your culture? On the other hand, a macho is someone who can and will take care of his family honorably.

Macchu Picchu: This is the mountain we climb to be a man. The boy dies so the man can be born. Or another way, Let the boy live, but let the man be stronger. We go up this mountain. We write our poems. This is the way of the abrecaminos. We only carry what we need. Break chains and get up the mountain.

madre: Mother. My mother is my treasure. The root of life.

Malinchista: Someone compared to Malinche. Traditionally called the betrayer, Malinche also has another tradition of being a pathbreaker, a multicultural, multilingual and political image in Mexican history.

maldición: Malediction, curse. We are not cursed.

Mestizaje: The being different in more than color and textual features. Knowing that "Raza" is but a title and standing within a stereotyped group. For being mestizo is but a lighter shade of brown, and we often forget we are all of color.

mano: Hand. Her hand touched my dream. Or, *Da me una mano*. Give me a hand.

mochila: Backpack. We don't carry anything in our backpacks we don't need.

modo de ser: Way to be. The poet Rosario Castellaños writes about *otro modo de ser*, another way to be.

molcajete: It is a kind of a small pot made of rock. It is used to grind tomatoes, peppers, cilantro, mixed with water and salt to create a hot sauce called salsa. Molar—grindar for the different spices and herbs.

mundo: World. The world is full of hatred. The world is full of love. Which world are we living in?

noche: Night. That night she left me under the darkness. Noche de pura vida y muerte.

olvidar: To forget. It is hard to forget the past. No se debe olvidar el pasado; solo con el pasado podemos sobrevivir.

oro: Gold. My parents are worth more than gold. Or, *hecho de oro*, we are made of gold.

orgullo: To demonstrate that you could feel better and not be hurt. Egoista. Demostrar realmente lo que sentimos. A state of mind. Happiness to be shown. Self-esteem. I think pride can over run those with weak hearts. Orgullo de ser quien eres: de lo que portas, de tu cultura y de tu gente. Y puedes perder mucho solo por ser orgulloso.

padre: Father. My father was never there for me. Now I find fathers in men everywhere. And this: Mi padre es mi ser, sin él cual, podría perecer, sin vivir mi vida ni la familia defender. Without him I wouldn't be able to do it.

pasado: Past. My life was in the past, but knowing my raices, my roots, I know myself.

patrón: The cacique, hacendado. The man at the rancho with the power. One of the reasons behind the Revolution was to get rid of the *patrón*. The boss.

pensar: To think. Every second I think of you. Siempre te tengo en mis pensamientos.

perder: To lose. We lose sometimes in life and we have to live with it.

poetry: Palabra de fuerza, potencia inalcansable, que sobre pasa las fronteras y derrota todas las barreras. It's the inside power we must show to cross borders and break chains. For me, it means part of my heart, desquitamos nuestro coraje cuando lo escribimos en poemas, is part of my life, a metaphor that deals with your perspective, imitating your world, the sight that we have everyday when we are trying to send ourselves forth in the world. Poetry brings the abrecaminos to life. A poet should able to live and understand all the different worlds.

pobre: Poor. Receive this poor man inside of you.

popis: Slang. A name that my mom, my sister and I thought about to name our little kitty when we had it in México. Actually, Popis is a name that we classify some persons acting really elegant in the way they talk and walk and move. Our kitty would sometimes act this way.

por: For. I will go back for her.

¿por qué?: Why? Why suffer for a love that I never knew?

profundo: Profound, deep. You are deep inside.

pueblo: Village, town. Comala, the white village of America.

querer: To like. To like is not the same as to love. Also, to desire. There is a famous *dicho*, *Querer es poder*, that means to want to do something is to be able to do it. Note: Querer is also used to mean to love, such as, *Te quiero mucho*.

quinceañera: Es cuando dejas la niñez y entras a mujer. At 15, the traditional passage from being a girl to becoming an adult.

ranchero: Farmworker. A person who works at a farm doing hard jobs. Also a farm owner.

rancho: Many of us come from the ranchos.

raza: Tu cultura, tu familia, tu lengua, tu color, tu sangre. Mi raza son los hispanos. José Vasconcelos, minister of education in México during the 19th Century, called us the Raza Cósmica, the new race of people for the world. One group fighting together for rights and freedom of their world. It's not a street gang. La raza es nuestro orgullo, las culturas de nuestros padres. Not one or the other, but the best of both.

realidad: Reality. I am afraid to find the reality.

recordar: To remember. I remember your beautiful face.

repartiendo leche: Milkman. A person who goes door by door selling milk, this can be seen in México.

resortera: It is kind of a sling shot. In some parts of México they still use it as a tool for hunting.

revolutíon: There has to be a revolution in every single person in the world. So you can realize life. Si no hubiera revolución en nuestras vidas, no tuvieramos ningún sentido.

río: River. The river is filled with my tears of sadness. We cross rivers.

It's one of our metaphors. Once you cross a river your world changes.

rosa: Rose. A rose died in my soul.

sentir: To feel. I want to feel the love within me. I want to feel like the wind. Quien siente como el viento. Non conformist.

silencio: La habilidad de podernos comunicar con nosotros mismos, Dios y la naturaleza de una forma profunda. através el silencio se llega a la iluminación. Silence brings us powerful knowledge, but we must learn to break the silence, too. You need to talk sometimes. You need to speak out or they will take advantage of you.

sol: Sun. The sun's brightness disappeared.

soledad: Solitude, loneliness. Estar solo no es malo, es un rato para reflexionar lo que has echo en tu vida. It's not bad. You learn what you've done in your life. Before you can live with someone else you have to live with yourself.

sólo: Alone, single. Sometime I feel alone when she is not with me.

sueño: dream. A dream is just a fantasy. Lost only to be found within heart. Dream dreams, see visions, speak in parables.

tiempo: time, epoch, period, season. It takes time to forget a true love.

tierra: land, sand. My land is México.

tortilla: Bread made of corn. In México, during prehispanic times, the Aztecs considered this food sacred, and to this time it is an important part of our diet.

tristeza: Sadness, gloom. My hands are covered with sadness. We have an expression, *la tristeza de la vida*, the sadness of life. La vida no es toda una alegría. Hay que conocer la tristeza para apreciar la alegría.

troje: A big home made of wood. It is usually constructed in rural places. In some places it is also used to store big amounts of grain. The church; the congregation of the faithful.

truth: La verdad. La verdad no peca, pero incomoda. Hay veces en que we have to say the truth. It makes people uncomfortable. The truth is something we say with certeza and sinceridad.

único: Only. My only dream is to help my family.

usted: You. You took my breath away.

venganza: Revenge. This is one of the cycles we break. How do you break this cycle in your culture? Es cuando tú le haces algo a otra persona porque ellos te hiceieron algo a ti.

vera: Edge, border. There are no borders between cultures, only challenges to be acted upon.

verdad: the truth. The truth is that I love you. See truth.

verde: Green. The yard is still green. Es el color principiante de todo lo que vive y nos sostiene.

vida: Life. Life has lots of traps.

viento: Wind. The wind doesn't takes the pain away, pero ayuda a desparramar la semilla de alegría. Then the wind makes everything clear again.

About the Authors

Sandra Abundiz: I am 18 years old. I graduated in the spring of 1998. My goals are to finish raising my daughter Xiemura Lozano and maybe later on go to college. I plan to get a job as a Dental Assistant and give my family the best I can. These stories are dedicated to my beautiful daughter Xiemura and my wonderful husband José Lozano.

Ricardo Acevedo: I've been raised by two hard working and loving parents. I've walked through streets of violence and through my parents' advice I've learned to stay away from bad stuff. Living in a bad neighborhood all my life has only made it harder for me, but I'm doing good. I have six brothers and two sisters all of who have been brought up the right way. I am proud of my parents. I now attend Davis High School, temporarily, because I plan to move on. (Ed. note: Ricardo Acevedo earned his diploma June, 1998.)

Gavicel Antúñez Torres: I'm the student of the Abrecaminos. I was born February 19, 1980 in Mexico City, Nezahualcoyotl, México. I have my mother and my father and my little brother and that's it, without them I'm nothing. I love painting and drawing and reading and I'm a dreamer. I write poems and stories and much more.

Tony Avila: ...is learning how to choose the right path. He learns how to write poems and tell stories about the past and present. I go to practice soccer mostly everyday—not when it rains, but when there is sunshine. I always say, "Living in the U.S. It's hard being Latino." Not married but planning in the future. I walk my dog, Lucky, to the Greenway Park. Lucky because my eyes were on him and for being part of my life since he was a puppy and he still is. I have to find him a female because I'm his friend and he needs a girlfriend.

Angel Ayon: My name is Angel Ayon. I am a dreamer. I have visions of beautiful lives. They are coming true through my poems. I write and I try to introduce myself to everyone. I am a poet of love. I work with the elderly. In my writing I'm trying to cause a revolution. In myself, and maybe in others. I am trying to be reached. I listen to music and <u>hear</u> it. I love to watch movies of all kinds. I pray every day for myself and those around me. I am not afraid because I am not alone. I dream of becoming a chemical engineer.

Samuel Barrera: I was born in Los Sauces, Guerrero, México. I'm a freshman at Heritage College. My career is to become a computer scientist. I believe that some place in my heart there is a light that will guide me through the days, whether they are bad or good. I think that every person has a heart, as well as many dreams, and any dream can become true with a beat of your heart and with a little bit of faith and trust in ourselves.

Adriana Cárdenas: I am an out going young woman full of life. I like to play soccer and basketball in my spare time, as well as write poetry. In my writing, I'm trying to find myself as well as my path for the future.

Maira Cárdenas: My name is Maira Cárdenas. I am a student at Davis High School. I power lift with Mr. Steele. I like to compete and now there's always something to improve. I like to travel and discover new things. I am a junior hoping to graduate next year.

Natalia Castañeda: I'm a student at Davis High School. I like to write stories, but fiction only. I live with my parents, my smart brother, and four sisters. We came to the United States *para abrir las puertas* (to open doors) *y descubrir barreras* (discover barriers). I like to go to the movies and have fun.

Salvador Castañeda Muñiz: Graduated from Davis High School in Yakima, WA. He likes to write about his past life experiences. He began attending the University of Washington on the fall of 1998 and major in Computer Engineering. His family migrated to the U.S. in 1982. Originally from Guadalajara, Jalisco México. Salvador is the oldest of his family which counts of five sisters, no brothers, and both his parents. He likes to be challenged in any way and enjoys lifting weights as a hobby.

Raúl Chacón: My name Is Raúl Chacón. I live in Naches WA. But I'm a student of Latino Literature at Davis High School. I describe myself as a friendly and peaceful person. I like to watch soccer and Argentina will be Champions in France 98 (World Cup). I also like to listen to music, to dance, to write poems and songs, to read the Bible and have fun whatever I go. One of the most interesting things about me is that I always take a shower. I am a thousand years old because I never count my age by years. I count it by friends.

Beatriz Díaz: I'm from Mexico City, D. F. I came to this country planning to study and learn more about the culture. I've been here for almost four years. At school everyday I attempt to absorb much of everything and know more about the people I share with everyday. My goal in life is to bring all my dreams to truth, and most special, to leave a wonderful message in this world, "Do not ever let your dreams vanish into the air." I like everything that has to do with books that talk about us (human beings). I live with my mom, Maria Ibarra, my brother, Israel and my older sister, Maria Díaz. We spend time together always and we enjoy what we always plan to do.

Berenice Garcia: I am currently a student at Davis High School. I like to sing and I just became interested in photography. I'd like to make it a hobby because it is a way of expressing feelings.

Jesús Gil: I am 17 years old. I'm attending Davis High School in Yakima WA. I am in the 11th grade. I am a person that likes the freedom to do whatever you want without offending others. I like the people who listen to the stories of others and try to help them. My favorite sport is to play soccer in my free times.

Angel González: I'm a happy guy and I like to hang with my friends, and to take care of my brothers and sisters. I also like to study and I'm proud of my parents because they give me their life, because without them I wouldn't survive and couldn't go ahead with their help. That's why I thank to God for giving me this graduation and this life.

Carlos A. Gonzalez: I'm an abrecaminos. I write poems where I tell how my life is. I like to make a way where there is no way. I'm looking for the American dream. I like to play basketball, to have things clean and organized. I lived 18 years of my life with my grandparents, and I came to the United States three years ago to live with my parents. In my writing I'm trying to tell my ups and downs, who I am and how I think about life.

Humberto Granados: I'm a student who also is a *abrecaminos*. I write poems and tell stories about my life. Sometimes I make a way where there is no way. I look for myself between poems, stories and dreams. I like to play soccer at anytime and anywhere with my friends. When I'm not playing or studying I clean up the yard and my room. If I don't have anything to do I talk on the phone or watch TV.

René Guzmán: My name is René Guzmán. I'm a student at Davis High School. I like to write poems about everything but especially about love. I live with my parents, they are proud of me for getting good grades at school. I'm a Junior with 17 years old. I like romantic music, and I spend time with my friends, playing soccer. When I write my pen is my voice.

Jacqueline Hernández: I just got married, December 18, 1998. I am attending Yakima Valley Community College and I'm planning to get an accounting degree. I am going to get a house for my future children. My goal right now is to get a good job and live well for the rest of my life and be as happy as I can be. I was born in Watsonville, California in 1978, but I grew up in a little town in Jalisco, México, nearby the Lago de Chapala, a very famous and beautiful lake. I lived there from the age of two until I was fourteen, when I came to the United States to study.

Pablo López: I'm a student at Davis High School. Sometimes I write poems and stories, but what I really like is to play soccer or any other sport. I work at Top Foods after school, and I like to spend time with my friends because when we all get together we start to play soccer and we start to have fun. I am from México.

Rubén Mendoza: I am the author of the poem, "The Curves of My Life." I wrote this poem about three years ago. It is about something that happened to me and my family. It affected us all very deeply when we were young and we didn't understand what was happening at that time. Today all grown up, I understand and remember, and I will never forget. Today I live with my father, my sisters and my brother. I like to go to the movies and watch sports. I also work and help my family. I am not married but I hope I will be someday.

Juan Ortega: My memories are a buildup of anger in a day to day search for some truth. Something while living to get. In my youth, life is consumed by figuring out what to do. Every fork in the road splits me in two for I'm still trying to do it all. My satisfaction lies in achieving success, for Mom, brothers and friends. The anxiety of this keeps me awake nights. In the age of governments, I govern myself. I was born in Puebla, México, in 1978. I came to the U. S. as a 1 1/2 year old infant. I grew up in Torrance, California, until the age of 13. We moved to Portland. I moved to Deutschland. I lived with my brother and his wife and two kids. I moved to Yakima in 94 to live with my Mom and stepdad in the blistering heat and misery.

Martha Ponce: I came from a family of 9 children and my two parents. I'm a senior at Davis High School. I graduate on June 6th and I feel really proud of myself. For me Davis High School was the best high school and the teacher I got to know were a really big help and I'm glad to have known them. I like to write a lot, and listen to music when I'm writing. I love to dance. I'm from Mexico City and I have studied here in the U.S. since 4th grade.

Omar Ramírez: My name is Omar Ramírez Cruz, I am a formal student at A.C. Davis High School, in Yakima, Washington. My Latino Literature teacher found my stories and my poems by a salty coast while

I was hidden in an isolated galaxy away from the human being. I was scared to be a part of your society. This writing has taught me how to be someone in this bitter life and how to be an *abrecamino*. My mother, Celsa, has been my only parent. She has struggled in life to give to my brother and sister and me the illusion in her vast dream underneath that black moon that we stare at every night. She is the most important person in my poor life. Thanks to her I have opened my own journey into your bright world. As a handicapped person with cerebral palsy, I had learned my grief, my sorrow, *y sobre todo la cruel realidad* to accept myself. To some people I am the "Retarded Kid" who doesn't have the clue about life, who has been given the restrictions of love, or the "bohemian on desert sands". In reality I'm the wayfarer on your roads without a course to follow. All I have are my roses and my thorns to give to the beautiful public. My God wanted me like this for a reason, no one can act against His will, thanks to Him we are here to suffer like he did. The hope will blossom by your eyes. Thanks for the permission to plant my vein in everyone's minds.

Juan Romo: I came from Cd. Juarez, Chihuahua, México. I have been shown a new way. In my writing I'm trying to show all who doubt me and my people that we too can play a major role in society, not only as criminals, but as active contributors to literature, art and society as a whole. I enjoy listening to music and spending a lot of time with my Rottweilers. I'm also one of those people who help others find a way. In some cases we make a way if there's none available. I am also one of many in the family of abrecaminos, and together me and this family of helpers will continue now and forever to look for ways to help others.

Teresa Roque: I'm a student at Davis High School. I like to write what I feel. I'm 17 years old. I live with my parents. I have three brothers and one baby sister. My dream is to become a teacher. I thank everybody that helped me understand life better.

Gabino Salazar: Currently I am 19 years old, and a freshman in college. I like to enjoy soccer, basketball and I am very happy because in two months more I will get my Black Belt—well, if I pass the test. I am majoring in business and political science. Once I finish my four years of college I might go back to México and build my life there. I am the type of person that likes to dream, and I know that I can make my dreams come true because I trust and believe in myself.

Jorge Carlos Sanchez: The place where I was brought up was known as the Black Hole of Washington, or as some people call it, The Ghetto. As a boy, I was always around drugs and gangs. As I see it, the only way out of the ghetto was to express myself in art. My drawing represents that you don't know anyone until you look at their personality. What makes me who I am is the fact that I was brought up in the ghetto and people would call me a loser and that I was a no one. That is what made me a strong Mexican that will prove to those people that doubted me that I'm someone that will come up on top, someone that started at the bottom of a hole with gangs and drugs will end up on top, out of the hole.

Salvador Sanchez: I love to learn about my culture and literature. I love to do many things such as read, play sports, and use my computer in my spare time. Helping students and finding solutions for society is a priority to me because it makes me feel proud about myself. I'm planning on going to college and becoming an engineer or maybe perhaps a Latino Literature teacher. I have a family of eight.

Luis Solis: I'm a student at the University of Washington. I like to play many sports. I was very active in high school. I was on the varsity football team for 3 years. I was the inspiration and academic player in 1997. I was a member at A.C. Davis chapter at National Honor Society. I was student of the month on several occasions. I am part of the 1997 edition of student selected as who's who among American High School Students. I was the first person to graduate from High School from family. I will become the first college grad of my family. I plan to be an engineer. I plan to succeed.

Siddhartha Eva Valdivia. I named myself. I've been an *"abrecamino"* since I joined the Latino Literature class. I find myself deep inside and break the chains to break away. I observe and listen. I also make a way where there is no way. I seek. I dance and become part of a different world. A world of passion peace and pleasure. I enjoy debating and hearing different opinions. I no longer run, but be myself. I am in a journey. It feels great! I am all detail. I have a four year old daughter who I love with all my heart. She's my everyday inspiration to seek for the best! My dreams become accomplishments. My pain becomes my strength!

Cesar Vaquera: Living, learning, failing, prevailing with an artistic mind. I'm 20 years old. I'm a positive street dancer with the mentality of a lover and a fighter. Even though visions are blurry, like dreams, hate follows me like love, and everyday prayer is a must in my life. When I see art it amazes me, especially if I'm the creator. It can be stressful, like love.

Alma Varela: I graduated from Davis High School and I'm attending college. Living in México and the United States has made me feel at home, but as I grow older, I realize that life can be so tough and so unfair that it can leave you homeless. So I've learned that life itself is a home. I like to remember my childhood and my people because it wakens me into a new dream. It's hard for us Mexicans to make our way into the United States, but it makes us tougher and smarter. My biggest dream in life is to have the strength to continue dreaming. I have many chllenges and goals in my life but I work and pray to succeed.

Rafael Villalobos: Like my father, I carry "la sangre de Indio" in my veins. Hoping to one day pass it down, across or over, even through, to another individual. Precious land of grace and beauty. It has given me so much, and taken even more. I seem to be in debt, and until the sun falls in the West as I perish, shall my bill be sealed and paid for. The hand that feeds us is the same to make me cry. I envy those that have what I remember from some time ago: Unity, love under a roof, one whole in many parts. In my writing I'm trying to express my proudness of who I am, tell about America, the woman I love and/but shall never have. Her parents are closed as mine are, always at war. I have a lot, but always wish I could have what I need, not want, like someone to share my every thought with, a person to hold me, and not let me die.

Jim Bodeen

Jorge Sanchez

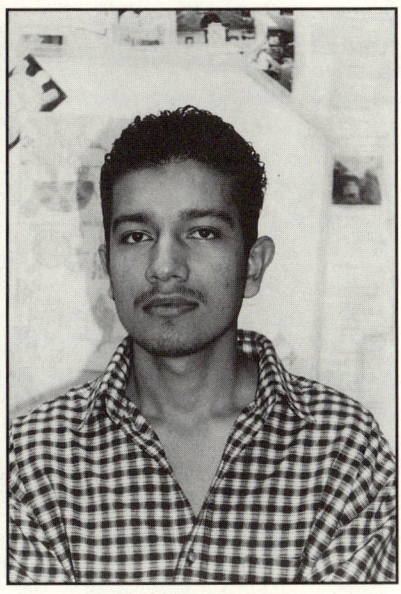

Javier Vargas

Rafael Villalobos

Cesar Vaquera